SERVANT Leaders

13 Fun Filled Bible Lessons About Serving God

Susan L. Lingo

STANDARD PUBLISHING™

Cincinnati, Ohio

DEDICATION

Serve one another in love.
Galatians 5:13

Servant Leaders
© 2000 Susan L. Lingo

Published by Standard Publishing, Cincinnati, Ohio
A division of Standex International Corporation

Credits

Produced by Susan L. Lingo, Bright Ideas Books™
Cover design by Diana Walters
Illustrated by Marilynn G. Barr and Megan E. Jeffery

07 06 05 04 03 02 01 00 5 4 3 2 1
ISBN 0-7847-1147-X
Printed in the United States of America

CONTENTS

SECTION 1: A SENSE OF SERVING

SECTION 2: SERVANT LEADERS IN THE OLD TESTAMENT

SECTION 3: SERVANT LEADERS IN THE NEW TESTAMENT

SECTION 4: SERVING TODAY!

SERVANT LEADERS REVIEW LESSON (Colossians 3:17)

INTRODUCTION

POWERING UP YOUR KIDS' FAITH!

Congratulations! You're about to embark on a wonderful mission to strengthen, energize, and stabilize your kids' faith and fundamental knowledge of God—faith and fundamentals that will launch your kids powerfully into the twenty-first century!

Servant Leaders is part of the Power Builders Series, an exciting and powerfully effective curriculum that includes *Value Seekers*, *Faith Finders*, *Disciple Makers*, and *Servant Leaders*, the book you're now holding.

Servant Leaders is dedicated to building and reinforcing kids' faith so they can serve and live in today's—and tomorrow's—world. Thirteen theme-oriented lessons will help your kids discover why they should serve, how men and women in the Old and New Testaments served God in various ways, and how they can serve God and others today. In addition, woven throughout each lesson is Scripture, Scripture, and more Scripture!

Each lesson in *Servant Leaders* has the following features:

POWER FOCUS (Approximate time: 10 minutes)—You'll begin with a mighty motivator to get kids thinking about the focus of the lesson. This may include an eye-popping devotion, a simple game, or another lively attention-getting tool. Included is interactive discussion and a brief overview of what kids will be learning during the lesson. *Purpose: To focus attention and cue kids in to what they'll be learning during the lesson.*

MIGHTY MESSAGE (Approximate time: 15 minutes)—This is the body of the lesson and includes engaging Bible passages that actively teach about the lesson's theme. The Mighty Message is not just "another Bible story," so your kids will discover God's truths through powerful passages and important portions of Scripture that are supported by additional verses and made relevant to kids' lives. Processing questions help kids explore each side of the passages and their relation to the theme, beginning with easier questions for young children and ending with more challenging think-about-it questions for older kids. Meaty and memorable, this lesson section will help kids learn tremendous truths! *Purpose: To teach powerful biblical truths and offer thought-provoking discussion in age-appropriate ways.*

MESSAGE IN MOTION (Approximate time: 10-15 minutes)—This section contains engaging activities that enrich and reinforce the lesson theme. It may include creative crafts, lively games and relays, action songs and rhythmic raps, mini service projects, and much more. *Purpose: To enrich learning in memorable and fun ways that build a sense of community.*

SUPER SCRIPTURE (Approximate time: 10-15 minutes)—This all-important section encourages and helps kids effectively learn, understand, and apply God's Word in their lives. The Mighty Memory Verse was chosen so every child can effectively learn it during the course of three weeks, but an extra-challenge verse is offered for older kids or children who can handle learning more verses. You are free to substitute your own choice of verses in this section, but please keep in mind that the activities, songs, crafts, and mnemonic devices are designed for the Mighty Memory Verse and the accompanying extra-challenge verse. And remember, when it comes to learning God's Word, effective learning takes place when kids work on only one or two verses over the course of several weeks! *Purpose: To memorize, learn, recall, and use God's Word.*

POWERFUL PROMISE (Approximate time: 5-10 minutes)—The lesson closes with a summary, a promise, and a prayer. You'll summarize the lesson, the Mighty Memory Verse, and the theme, then challenge kids to make a special commitment to God for the coming week. The commitments are theme-related and give kids a chance to put their faith into action. Finally, a brief prayer and responsive farewell blessing end the lesson. *Purpose: To make a commitment of faith to God and express thanks and praise to him.*

POWER PAGE! (Take-home paper)—Each lesson ends with a fun-to-do take-along page that encourages kids to keep the learning going at home. Scripture puzzles, crafts, recipes, games, Bible read-about-its, Mighty Memory Verse reinforcement, and more challenge kids through independent discovery and learning fun. *Purpose: To reinforce, review, and enrich the day's lesson and the Mighty Memory Verse.*

PLUS, in every Power Builder's book you'll discover these great features!

★ **WHIZ QUIZZES!** At the end of each section is a reproducible Whiz Quiz to gently, yet effectively, assess what has been learned. Completed by kids in about five minutes at the end of lessons 3, 6, 9, and 12, the Whiz Quiz is a nonthreatening and fun measuring tool to allow teachers, kids, and parents to actually see what has been learned in the prior weeks. When kids complete each Whiz Quiz, consider presenting them a collectible surprise such as a vase and silk flowers that represent how God's truth and love are growing and flowering in their lives. For example, after the first Whiz Quiz, present each child with a small bud vase After the next Whiz Quiz, present a red silk flower. Then use blue and yellow flowers for lessons 9 and 12. When the book is complete, kids will have an entire bouquet that they can then give to someone else as an act of loving service. Kids will love the cool reminders of the lessons and their accomplishments! Be sure to keep children's completed Whiz Quiz pages in folders to present to kids at the end of the book or at the end of the year, in combination with other Whiz Quizzes from different books in the Power Builders Series.

★ **LESSON 13 REVIEW!** The last lesson in *Servant Leaders* is an important review of all that's been learned, applied, accomplished, and achieved during the past twelve weeks. Kids will love the lively review games, action songs, unique review tools, and celebratory feel of this special lesson!

★ **SCRIPTURE STRIPS!** At the back of the book, you'll discover every Mighty Memory Verse and extra-challenge verse that appears in *Servant Leaders*. These reproducible Scripture strips can be copied and cut apart to use over and over for crafts, games, cards, bookmarks, and other fun and fabulous "you-name-its"! Try gluing these strips to long Formica chips to make colorful, clattery key chains that double as super Scripture reviews!

★ **TEACHER FEATURE!** Discover timeless teaching tips and hints, hands-on help, and a whole lot more in this mini teacher workshop. Every book in the Power Builders series offers a unique Teacher Feature that helps leaders understand and teach through issues such as discipline, prayer, Scripture memory, and more. The Teacher Feature in *Servant Leaders* is "A Realistic Look at Rewards."

God bless you as you teach with patience, love, and this powerful resource to help launch kids into another century of love, learning, and serving God! More POWER to you!

A REALISTIC LOOK AT REWARDS

Let's get real ... how many adults go to work each day and put in long, arduous hours from the goodness of their hearts, expecting no monetary reward for their labors? Probably few, if any. After all, this is the real world, and our society is built upon a financial system that requires the reward of paychecks to function.

But what about the controversy over using positive rewards in classrooms? Is it real to think kids have inherent, intrinsic drives—or do they need a boost to modify behavior, encourage learning, and set goals? Well, what does the Bible say about rewards? Plenty! Hebrews 11:6 says, "Without faith it is impossible to please God, because anyone who comes to him must believe that he exists and that he rewards those who earnestly seek him." Likewise, 1 Samuel 26:23 states that "the Lord rewards every man for his righteousness," while in Luke 6:23 Jesus says, "Rejoice in that day and leap for joy, because great is your reward in heaven."

Reward is nothing new in the Bible or in today's classrooms, though many teachers worry that rewarding kids for behavior or learning gives a wrong message about goals. Edward L. Thorndike, a prominent child psychologist, prefers to address reward as "operant learning," that is, learning in order to gain positive responses, which tend to increase learning. This is where intrinsic and extrinsic rewards come in. When kids or adults regard learning as pleasurable and something good in and of itself, they are motivated intrinsically and want to learn more. But if a child does not perceive the inherent value in a lesson, learning becomes difficult and unmotivated. This explains why many teachers use extrinsic rewards to boost kids' motivation. The rewards help kids develop positive views of learning as something pleasurable and good, which creates the intrinsic motivation to want to learn more.

Elementary-aged children, not to mention even younger kids, have a difficult time perceiving much of the Bible and God's Word as inherently pleasurable, valuable, or good. They may need the boost of extrinsic rewards in areas such as Scripture memory or daily Bible reading. Many teachers wonder, "Should I offer a piece of candy, a sticker, or other small reward for learning

Scripture verses? Shouldn't kids just naturally *want* to learn God's Word?" First of all, we can't put a value on God's Word, though it most certainly is worth a piece of candy or a sticker. If that's all it takes, great! Why wouldn't we want to encourage kids to learn God's Word at *any* cost?

Second, it *would* be wonderful if all kids were intrinsically motivated to learn or read the Bible, but that is contrary to how children function at an early age. They are simply unable to understand how learning a verse today will affect their eternal spirits tomorrow and beyond. Kids learn in concrete, nonconceptual ways. How, then, can we expect young children to be motivated solely by ethereal, spiritual promises?

Dr. Walter B. Kolesnik states, "It is considerably easier to motivate a person toward an immediate rather than a delayed reward. One of the signs of maturation is a person's willingness to work for a delayed reward."

Until young children are able to make the jump to intrinsic motivation and are able to view life beyond their own short years, they will probably need external, extrinsic boosts. Rather than denying this important tool for helping kids make the transition to intrinsic drive, perhaps we should look at reward from the standpoint of *how* to reward and *what* rewards are suitable for giving kids positive messages.

Positive Motivation and How to Use It

Many teachers prefer to view reward in terms of the action it accomplishes: positive motivation. Used as a reinforcement for positive behavior, learning, and "just because" times, positive motivation keeps kids challenged and with a positive, anticipatory attitude. Using positive motivation is also a wonderful way to teach grace and goal setting. And positive reinforcement is very effective when used as affirmations in the form of notes, hugs, smiles, and rewarding words of praise. Here are a few use-them-now ideas to implement positive motivation in your classroom.

★ **GIFTS OF GRACE** (Ephesians 2:4, 5)—Small "just because" rewards are a boost and a lift to kids ! Choose a day to reward your kids "just because," then hand out small items such as homemade cookies, note pads, tiny Bibles, or even flowers. Explain that God gives us the gift of grace when we don't deserve it, which is what makes it so wonderful. Point out that you just wanted to reward kids for being the great people God is making them to be. Then stand back and watch the smiles! Use this reward for "just because" affirmations, attitude boosters, and motivators.

★ **HAVE A HEART JAR** (Luke 6:23)—Fill a large, clear jar with candy hearts or chocolate kisses. Then hand each child an index card. Instruct kids to draw five or ten heart outlines on their cards and write their names at the tops of the cards.

Explain that over the next five (or ten) class periods, they'll be reading (or memorizing) verses from the Bible about love, kindness, and how we're to treat others. After each reading or repetition of Scripture, have kids color in a heart. When the cards are colored, let kids choose a candy treat from the jar. Be sure to point out that, although it's fun to have an occasional treat, God's Word is an everlasting treat! Use this reward to motivate kids to set and reach both short-term and long-term learning goals.

★ **HOLD THAT HAPPY FACE!** (Ephesians 2:8, 9)—Draw three happy faces on an index card for each child. Let kids write their names on the cards, then tape the cards to tables, desks, or the door. Explain that kids have already been given three happy faces and that their goal is to have at least one happy face left at the end of the day, week, or month. When you observe negative behavior (be sure to give specific examples), you'll simply cross off a happy face, but kids will still have the choice of keeping two more. Point out how God's grace is given (not earned) and how it's our decision how we react to it. In the same way, it's each person's decision how to react to the happy faces and what choices are made to keep them. At the end of the specified time, offer a small treat to anyone with one or more happy faces unmarked. Use this reward for behavior modification, focusing kids' attention, and setting goals.

Stickers, Stamps, and Other Rewards

Now that we've discovered that it's okay and even beneficial to use positive rewards in class, what kinds of rewards are there? Which rewards will motivate young kids to learn without drawing their focus away from why they're learning? Let's take a look at three types of rewards and how each fits into the classroom!

1. CONCRETE REWARDS—These are rewards kids can see, feel, hold, and recognize with perceived value. Paul spoke of concrete rewards or prizes in 1 Corinthians 9:24 and Philippians 3:14. The Greek word for prize, *brabeion,* has in mind a "prize or award in a contest." In biblical days, Paul was familiar with sporting events in which victors were awarded palm branches and small crowns (2 Timothy 4:7, 8). He wanted us to know that we're to strive for our upward prize in Jesus the same as we would strive for a prize in a race or contest.

Kids enjoy the challenge of working for concrete items, and though they may not fully understand the more ethereal reasons for learning biblical truths and verses, they do realize that they're important enough to strive for if a reward of sorts is involved. As kids mature, the need for concrete rewards lessens but still doesn't disappear completely. After all, even 1 Timothy 5:18 says, "The worker

deserves his wages." *Concrete rewards: small erasers, pencils, homemade items,
cheery notes, hugs, note pads, Scripture verses in pretty envelopes, small Bibles,
stickers, combs, key rings, balloons, and paper awards.*

2. EMOTIONAL REWARDS—Emotional rewards include those hugs and
affirmations that all of us need at one time or another. If you asked teachers why they teach, you'd probably hear, "It makes me feel good" or "I
feel great serving God!" Even Jesus endured the cross because of the
joy that had been set before him (Hebrews 12:2)!

Some kids adore memorizing Scripture, and it seems to come easily for them because of their motivation. They enjoy knowing God's
Word and perhaps crave the affirmations they get from pastors, parents,
and teachers. Other kids, however, need a concrete reward to motivate them
to complete a series of verses. Which is best: intrinsic reward or extrinsic
reward? Neither! Both groups of kids are winners because they're learning
God's Word! *Emotional rewards: affirmations, encouraging notes, pictures and
happy faces, smiles, pats on the back, cute cards, and hugs.*

3. SPIRITUAL REWARDS—"For the Son of Man is going to come in his
Father's glory with his angels, and then he will reward each person according
to what he has done" (Matthew 16:27). Thank you, Lord, that there will be a
reward at the end of our lives if we earnestly seek, obey, and love you and
others! Kids are only beginning to understand the eternal consequences of
what they're learning in Sunday school, but that doesn't mean that they can't
handle the idea of spiritual rewards or the concept of what God has planned
for us. On their own level, kids do understand that God is all-powerful and
that Jesus died for them. And kids can grasp that, because God is all-powerful,
he can reward and punish as his Word and will promise! It is hard to impress
upon kids at this early age the importance of intrinsic spiritual motivation, but
it will develop with age—trust God to work on his youngest treasures!
*Spiritual rewards: verses about Jesus and our salvation tied in scrolls with rib-
bons, tiny framed pictures of Jesus, and small crosses that glow in the dark.*

The real world—how awful it would be without the promise and hope of
God's grace, his gifts of forgiveness and love, and his special rewards! So the
next time you wonder whether or not to use rewards to motivate your kids to
deeper learning and a greater appreciation for God and his Word, just remember:
*Without faith it is impossible to please God, because anyone who comes to him
must believe that he exists and that he rewards those who earnestly seek him.*

(Hebrews 11:6)

A SENSE OF SERVING

Whatever you do, work at it
with all your heart, as
working for the Lord,
not for men.
Colossians 3:23

SERVE ONLY GOD!

We want to serve only God.

Daniel 6:1-28
Matthew 6:24; 25:40

SESSION SUPPLIES

★ Bibles
★ fresh, raw vegetables
★ a pitcher of water and paper cups
★ poster board and scissors
★ markers, tape, and paper
★ gift wrap and boxes with lids
★ tempera paint and paper towels
★ Styrofoam meat trays and newspapers
★ photocopies of Colossians 3:23 (page 127)
★ photocopies of the Power Page! (page 19)

MIGHTY [MEMORY VERSE]

Whatever you do, work at it with all your heart, as working for the Lord, not for men. Colossians 3:23

SESSION OBJECTIVES

During this session, children will
★ realize that we're to serve only God
★ recognize things that keep us from serving
★ learn the importance of serving God
★ discover ways to serve the Lord

BIBLE BACKGROUND

What a dilemma! You've caught your boss at work in an act of dishonesty that affects many people. Speaking the truth is the right thing to do, but it could cost you your position. What do you do? Ask Daniel! He was trapped in a den with his own lions, yet Daniel never stopped serving God and, in the end, was rewarded with his life! We have many masters in our lives, from jobs and family responsibilities to financial obligations and health worries. But though they may growl and snipe for our full attention, we don't need to be ruled by these false masters! If we choose to serve only God, the lions and other snarly beasts in our lives won't devour us. And like Daniel, we'll be able to proclaim, "My God, whom I serve continually, rescues me!"

Even kids have people and things in their lives that try to draw them away from serving or focusing on God. Toys, sports, heroes, hobbies, music stars, and more can lead kids' focus away from God just as money can lead adults from focusing on the Lord as their sole—and soul—master! Use this lesson to help kids realize that the only one we want to serve, focus on, and expend our energies toward is God.

POWER FOCUS

Gather kids at one end of the room and explain that you'll begin by playing a quick game of Either-Or. Say: **In this game, I'll read a sentence that gives you a choice. You decide which action you'll do, then follow the directions. Ready?**

Read the following either-or sentences and pause for kids to make their decisions and follow the actions:

★ *Either hop or tiptoe across the room.*

★ *Either whistle or laugh out loud.*

★ *Either give someone a hug or shake hands.*

★ *Either do two somersaults or take two hops backwards.*

★ *Either touch your toes or reach up high.*

★ *Either clap your hands or slap your knees.*

★ *Either sit down or jump up.*

★ *Either say the alphabet or recite your address.*

★ *Either crawl or walk to our starting place.*

When kids are gathered back at the starting place, say: **Wow! You had a lot of decisions to make!** Then ask:

★ **Why couldn't you do both actions at the same time in this game?**

★ **How is this like having to choose between serving God and serving someone or something else?**

★ **Which is best: to serve God or someone else? Explain.**

Say: **This was a game of fun choices, and whatever you decided to do turned out fine. But in real life we have an important decision to make: whether to serve God or serve someone or something else. And whatever we choose can make the difference between life and death!**

Today we're starting a whole new group of lessons all about serving and being leaders for God. In today's lesson, we'll be discovering why we can't serve two masters at once and which master is the best choice to serve. We'll begin a fun service project that will last for the next couple of weeks. And we'll also learn a new Mighty Memory Verse about serving and work-

ing for God. Right now, let's discover how one fellow from the Bible chose to serve only God in a wonderful—but scary—way!

THE MIGHTY MESSAGE

Before class, prepare a plate of raw vegetables such as carrots, celery, broccoli, cucumbers, and radishes. (Cut a few extra vegetables widthwise and lengthwise to use in the Powerful Promise.) You may want to prepare veggie dip by stirring 2 teaspoons of prepared mustard into ½ cup mayonnaise. You'll also need a pitcher of water and paper cups. Set the vegetables, water, and cups on a table at one end of the room to be used at the right time in the story.

Gather kids in the center of the room and say: **Our Bible story today is from the book of Daniel in the Old Testament. It's about how Daniel chose to serve only one master—God! You can help act out the story as I retell it. When you hear the name *Daniel*, point upward and say, "I choose to serve God!"**

A long time ago, there was a young man named *Daniel*. *Daniel* loved God and wanted to serve only God in everything he said and did. Nothing could keep *Daniel* from serving God—and only God! Now *Daniel* lived in Babylonia, where the people didn't worship God. They worshiped idols and graven images and didn't love God at all. *Daniel* was supposed to be loyal to and serve King Nebuchadnezzar, but *Daniel* knew he could only be loyal to one master at a time, and that was to God!

When the king wanted *Daniel* to eat the food on his royal table, *Daniel* didn't want to eat what a king who didn't love God would eat. So *Daniel* asked to be given nothing but raw vegetables and water for ten days to show he could still be healthy. *Daniel* ate the vegetables and drank the water and stayed healthy and loyal to one master—God! Invite kids to choose and nibble one raw vegetable and sip a bit of water, then continue. (Assure kids they'll finish the treats later!)

Then a new king named Darius was crowned, and he made an awful law! It said that everyone had to pray to the king and no one else! *Daniel* refused to pray to anyone but God. That's because *Daniel* knew that he

POWER POINTERS

Kids often become too focused on sports heroes and music stars. Tell them that it's fine to appreciate talent, but we want to focus our energies on God and no one else!

could serve only one master—and he chose to serve God! King Darius told *Daniel* to pray to him or face the lions' den. **What do you think *Daniel* chose to do?** Pause for kids to tell their ideas, then say: *Daniel* **chose to serve God by praying to only him! "May your God, whom you serve continually, rescue you!" shouted the king. And King Darius tossed *Daniel* into the lions' den!**

Lead kids in growling like lions, then say: **All night, *Daniel* faced those lions. But *Daniel* didn't stop praying to God, and God heard his prayers. God sent an angel to close the mouths of the lions, and *Daniel* was saved! King Darius proclaimed God's power and said that people could pray to God after all! *Daniel* had stayed loyal to God and served only one master, the right master—God!** Invite children to gather around the table and munch the raw vegetables as you ask:

★ **Why was Daniel's decision to serve only God the right decision even though he faced a dangerous den of lions?**

★ **What might have happened if Daniel had tried to serve two masters at once: both King Darius and God?**

★ **What lesson can we learn from Daniel about serving only one master and making sure that master is God?**

★ **In what ways can you choose to serve only God?**

Say: **Because Daniel loved God so much, he wanted to serve only him, even though it meant he would face a den full of lions! Daniel showed us how important it is to serve just one master—God! The Bible tells us about serving one master.** Read aloud Matthew 6:24, then ask:

★ **What are other masters we serve besides money?**

★ **Why can't we serve two masters at one time?**

★ **In what ways does serving God make our lives easier? safer?**

★ **How does serving only God show him our love? our loyalty?**

Say: **The Bible says that if we try to serve two masters, we will love the one and grow to hate the other. Let's be sure the master we serve is God and only God! Because we love God, we choose to serve only him. Now let's learn more about serving God by starting work on a special project.** Have kids clean up any remaining snacks and toss their paper cups in the trash.

THE MESSAGE IN MOTION

Before class, collect a box and lid for every three kids. You'll also need a variety of festive gift wrap and plenty of clear tape. If you're presenting this lesson close to Valentine's Day, collect empty heart-shaped candy boxes—the kind with ribbons and ruffles. This service project will continue over the next two weeks and provide kids a chance to share their love and God's message of love and serving with others.

Have kids form trios and hand each group a box. Explain that this is a service project they will work on for three weeks to give everyone a chance to serve God through serving others. Say: **The Bible tells us a lot about serving. We just discovered that we can't serve two masters at one time. And we've learned that God is the master we choose to serve. Now listen to what the Bible says about doing things for others.** Read aloud Matthew 25:40, then ask:

★ **What do you think this verse is telling us?**

Say: **This verse tells us that when we serve others and help or do things for them, we're also serving God. That's pretty awesome, isn't it? Just think, when we serve others, we're serving God! Let's serve God by serving others with a sweet project. We'll make special Sweet Service Candy Boxes to give to others to remind them of God's love, our love, and how sweet it is to serve. This week we'll decorate the boxes.**

Decide who will receive the candy boxes. Suggestions might include people who need a special lift, Sunday school leaders who deserve a thank-you, or church helpers who are often unrecognized, such as secretaries or custodians.

Have kids cover the boxes and lids with wrapping paper. If you collected boxes that are already decorated on the outside, invite kids to embellish the insides. As kids work, encourage them to chat about times they've helped others and how they helped God at the same time. Ask kids how God feels when someone is happy we served them.

When the boxes are decorated, invite groups to display their handiwork. Encourage everyone to give a round of applause in appreciation for a job well done. Then say: **We'll keep our boxes here and add to them next week. You really worked hard decorating those boxes, and they're beautiful! Serving others isn't always easy, is it? But when we serve others, we're serving God, too—and that's worth all the hard work. Let's learn a new Mighty Memory Verse about working for the Lord.**

SUPER SCRIPTURE

Before class cut out a giant heart from poster board. Write the Mighty Memory Verse (Colossians 3:23) on the heart, making sure to include the Bible reference. Then cut the heart into six large pieces and set one piece aside when kids assemble the rest of the puzzle during the activity. You'll also need a photocopy of Colossians 3:23 from page 127 for each child, plus a copy for every three kids.

Have kids get in pairs or trios and hand each small group a puzzle piece. (If your class is larger than twenty-four kids, either make two puzzles or cut the heart into a few more pieces.) Explain to kids that you'll give them a few minutes to cooperatively assemble the puzzle. Tell children that the shape of the puzzle represents how we feel when we serve God.

After the heart is assembled (except for the "missing piece"), gather kids in front of the puzzle and ask:

★ **What shape is our puzzle?**

★ **What's missing in our puzzle? How does that affect the puzzle?**

★ **How is this puzzle like serving God with only a portion of our love or energy?**

Say: **This heart represents the love we feel for God when we serve him or serve others. But sometimes we don't serve God with all our hearts. Maybe we're too busy or not sure if we're serving the right way. God wants us to serve him just as we love him—with all our hearts!** Tape the missing puzzle piece in place.

Read the Mighty Memory Verse aloud, then have kids repeat the verse with you three times. Say: **Our Mighty Memory Verse reminds us how we're to serve the Lord all the time—working for God, not for the approval of others.** Ask:

★ **Why do we want to work for God and give him our very best?**

★ **How does working for God with all our hearts show our love?**

Say: **God deserves our very best. And whether we're serving, loving, worshiping, or praising God, we want to do it with all our hearts. Let's add the Mighty Memory Verse to the Sweet Service Candy Boxes to remind others that their work can be a work of love, too!**

Have kids cut out the Scripture strip for Colossians 3:23 and tape or glue it to the side of their project boxes. Then hand each child a copy of the Mighty Memory Verse to take home and practice. Say: **Learning God's Word is a way to serve God—and yes, it's work! But it's worth the time and effort we put into it. Practice your Mighty Memory Verse each day this week and remember that the work you're doing to learn God's Word is some-**

thing to be done with all your heart! Now let's discover another way we can serve God with all our hearts.

A **POWERFUL** PROMISE

Before class, cover a table with newspapers. Place paper towels in the bottoms of Styrofoam meat trays and pour a bit of paint on the paper towels to act as "ink pads." Use raw vegetable halves as "printers."

Have kids sit in a circle and ask for a moment of silence, then say: **We learned today that we can serve only one master and that we choose God as the only one to serve. We've also discovered that serving others and learning God's Word are ways to serve God. And we've worked on the Mighty Memory Verse that teaches us how we're to serve God. Colossians 3:23 says** (pause and invite kids to repeat the verse with you), **"Whatever you do, work at it with all your heart, as working for the Lord, not for men."**

Hold up the Bible and say: **God promises to help us serve him and others. Let's make a promise of our own to God. We can each commit to looking for ways to serve God this week with all our hearts. As we pass the Bible around our circle, we can say, "I will serve you, God."** Pass the Bible until everyone has had a chance to make a promise. End with a prayer asking for God's help in serving with all your hearts in all you do.

Have kids find places to stand around the table. (If you want kids to wear paint shirts, simply cut arm holes in paper grocery bags, then cut one side top to bottom to make disposable vests.) Hand kids paper and have them use markers to write "I will serve God with all my heart!" in the center of the paper. Then let kids make heart outlines around the words with vegetable prints.

I will serve God with all my heart!

When the pictures are finished, say: **Hang these special reminders of how Daniel served God in your room. When you read the words, thank God for his help in keeping our hearts strong and focused on serving him!** End with this responsive good-bye:

Leader: **May you always serve God.**

Children: **And also you!**

Distribute the Power Page! take-home papers as kids are leaving. Thank children for coming and encourage them to keep their promises to God this week.

POWER PAGE!

Serving Is No Puzzle!

1. Opposite of "go" is: _ _ _ O

2. To help someone: _ _ O _ _ _

3. End of a prayer: O _ _ _

4. Not me, but: O _ _

5. A lion's home: _ _ O _

6. Our mighty helper: _ _ O

Write the circled letters in order to discover how Daniel served God.

_ _ _ _ _ _

DANiEL'S LiONS

Daniel ate a healthy diet as a way to honor God. Make this healthful snack to stop your tummy from growling—and that's no "lion"!

You'll need:
- ★ raisins
- ★ dried, candied cherries
- ★ refrigerator biscuits

Directions:

Place nine of the biscuits on a cookie sheet. Use the extra biscuit to make ears and a mane on the other biscuits. Add raisins for eyes and candied cherries for noses and mouths. Bake at 350 degrees for 10 minutes or until golden brown. Cool and enjoy!

High & LOW

Use Colossians 3:23 to fill in the missing high and low letters. The first letter is done for you.

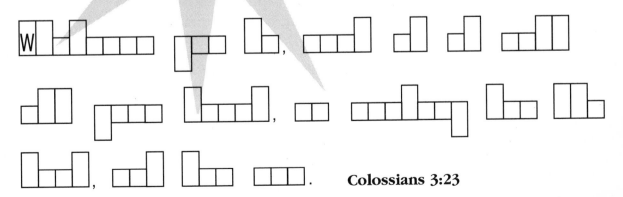

Colossians 3:23

SERVICE WITH A SMILE

Elijah

When we serve others, we're serving God.

1 Kings 17:1-16
Galatians 5:13

SESSION SUPPLIES

★ Bibles
★ paper towels
★ a box of soda or graham crackers
★ two grocery sacks
★ candy papers
★ tape, markers, and scissors
★ several bags of wrapped candies
★ newsprint and construction paper
★ photocopies of the Sweet Scriptures (page 123)
★ photocopies of the Power Page! (page 27)

MIGHTY MEMORY VERSE

Whatever you do, work at it with all your heart, as working for the Lord, not for men. Colossians 3:23

(For older kids, add in Galatians 5:13b: "Serve one another in love.")

SESSION OBJECTIVES

During this session, children will
★ recall that serving others is a way to serve God
★ realize that God helps us serve him
★ explore ways to serve other people
★ thank God for his love and help

BIBLE BACKGROUND

"I just can't find the time!" "It's not that I don't want to, but what can I do?" "Me, serve? I'll leave that to the missionaries at church!" Ahh, the excuses we find when called upon for help! Perhaps no other word makes people (including many Christians!) squirm like the word *service*. A million reasons why we can't, a thousand excuses why we won't—and one perfect reason why we should ... God! God calls us to serve others, and though we think we're not suited for the job, in fact we're all likely candidates for God's "selective service" positions! Take, for example, the widow in the story of Elijah from 1 Kings 17. She wasn't wealthy by any means, didn't have the one thing Elijah needed, and wasn't even an Israelite—but God used her to serve Elijah, her son, and himself in a powerful way through selfless serving! An unlikely candidate for serving? Perhaps by human definition. An unlikely candidate for serving God? There's no such thing!

Kids especially feel that they're unable to serve or to make a difference in someone's life. Too small, too young, too short, and limited by a fixed income (or allowance)—but kids can serve God and others in powerful ways they may not have thought of! Use this lesson to raise kids' awareness of what serving others means and to help them recognize that God intends to use them in just as many powerful ways as he does adults! When it comes to serving God, there are no age limits in signing on for the job!

POWER FOCUS

Before class, place the box of crackers on a table and the paper towels at another location. Remove about half the crackers and place them in the secret sack for The Mighty Message.

As kids arrive, greet them warmly, then invite them to sit in a circle. Sit down with the kids, then sigh and say: **Oh my! I forgot to bring something to our circle. Could I have a helper get the paper towels over there?** Point to the paper towels, then ask a child to bring them to you. Then say: **Thank you so much. But you know, I also forgot to bring over the crackers! Is there someone else who could get the crackers for me?** Again, ask a child to retrieve the crackers and bring them to the circle. Then say: **What a great help you all are and such willing servants! Now I have something for you that will help us begin our lesson for the day!**

Ask a child to deliver a cracker on a paper towel to another child you name. Then ask someone else to deliver another cracker and so on until everyone has had a turn to deliver a cracker and has received one. Then say: **Wow! You all pitched in so nicely with help. Now maybe you can help answer a few questions!** As kids nibble their crackers, ask:

★ **Who was being served when the paper towels and crackers were brought over? Explain.**

★ **In what ways were you serving your friends? serving me?**

★ **How is this like serving God when we're serving someone else?**

Say: **When you helped me by delivering the crackers and by getting the paper towels, you were really helping everyone in our classroom.**

That's pretty neat, isn't it? And that's how it is when we serve other people. When we serve others, we're serving God, too! It's like a super bonus—serving two or more at the same time!

Today we'll be exploring ways to serve others and how serving other people is serving God, too. We'll add to the Sweet Service Candy Boxes that we started last week and also review our Mighty Memory Verse, which teaches us, "Whatever you do, work at it with all your heart, as working for the Lord, not for men." But right now, let's jump into a great Bible story, and we'll learn how a man served God and a hungry widow and her son in an amazing way!

THE MIGHTY MESSAGE

POWER POINTERS

Help young kids understand that "serving" doesn't just mean giving someone a plate of food. It means anything we do to help them!

Before class, prepare a special bag by cutting one side from a grocery sack and taping it to the inside of another paper bag to make a secret compartment or pocket. (See illustration below.) Place one or two crackers for each child in the secret compartment and one cracker at the bottom of the sack. The sack should now appear to hold only one cracker. During the activity, you'll be showing kids the "empty" sack, so be sure to hold the top of the secret compartment closed as you tip the bag so kids can take a quick peek inside.

Set the sack in front of you and invite kids to tell about times they've helped or served someone and what the result of their help was. Then say: **The Bible is full of examples of people serving and helping each other. These people realized that when we serve others, we're serving God, too. Elijah loved God and wanted to serve him in all things. I'm going to read a story that comes from 1 Kings 17 in the Old Testament. It's a story about Elijah, a widow—a woman with no husband—and their hungry stomachs. We'll use this sack to help tell the story.**

Read aloud 1 Kings 17:1-16 or use the text below. When the widow tells Elijah she has only enough flour and oil for a bit of bread, show kids the one cracker and remove it from the bag. When God supplies a never-ending jug of oil and flour, begin pulling crackers from the hidden compartment. Kids will be amazed at how many crackers come from an "empty" bag!

Elijah met a widow in the town of Zarephath. "Please bring me a drink of water and a small piece of bread," said Elijah to the widow. But the widow was very poor and told Elijah she had only enough oil and flour to make one small cake of bread for her and her son. (Show the single cracker inside the sack.) **But Elijah told the widow to prepare a small cake of bread for him anyway and make the rest for her and her son.**

What do you think the woman did? Did she choose to serve Elijah unselfishly or did she keep the bread for her son and herself? What would you do? Allow kids time to share their responses, then continue.

The widow chose to do what Elijah asked. She made Elijah a small cake of bread. (Pull the cracker out of the bag, then show kids the "empty" sack.) **Now my flour and oil are gone, thought the widow. But were they? No way! God knew the widow served Elijah and, in so doing, she also served God. And God miraculously supplied the widow with flour and oil every day so she never ran out!** Begin pulling crackers from the sack and handing them to the kids.

When all the crackers are distributed, let kids munch as you ask:

★ **In what ways did Elijah serve God? the widow? the widow's son?**

★ **In what ways did the widow serve Elijah? serve God?**

★ **How do you think God felt when the widow served Elijah? Explain.**

★ **What can we learn about serving others through this story?**

Say: **The widow unselfishly served Elijah, and in so doing, she also served God. And God helped the woman by continually filling up her flour and oil supply. That's pretty awesome! We can be like the widow and unselfishly serve others and God at the same time, too.** Ask:

★ **What are ways we can serve and help others?**

Say: **God wants us to serve others, and there are so many ways to do this. One way is through love.** Read aloud Galatians 5:13, then say: **God will help us find different ways to serve and help others. In fact, we can lovingly serve others right now. Let's continue to work on our Sweet Service Candy Boxes. And as we work for others, we can be sure we're working for God as well!**

THE MESSAGE IN MOTION

Before class, photocopy the Sweet Scriptures from page 123, one copy for every three children. Be sure you have a plentiful variety of wrapped candies to place in the candy boxes. Red and white striped mints, butterscotch drops, and other hard candies will work well and look festive inside the boxes!

Have kids get in their service-project groups from last week. Hand out the boxes begun last week, then hand each group a copy of the Sweet Scriptures handout. Tell kids that this week they'll be adding paper candy cups to their boxes, then placing folded Scripture verses in some of the cups and yummy candies in the others. Let groups place twenty-four to thirty paper candy cups in their boxes. Have kids cut apart the Sweet Scriptures and fold them to fit in the paper cups. For an extra treat, invite kids to choose one candy each to enjoy as they work.

As kids work, have them take turns reading the verses on the Sweet Scriptures handout aloud and explaining what they mean. Then discuss why serving others is serving God at the same time. Read aloud Matthew 25:40 as kids work and ask questions such as, "Why is it important to treat others as if they are Jesus?" and "How does serving others help spread God's love to them?"

When the boxes are filled with Scripture verses and colorful candies, say: **It's not only helpful to serve others, it's fun, too! And when we know that we serve God when we serve others, it's even sweeter! I'm so glad that God is the one we've chosen to serve, aren't you? Let's review our Mighty Memory Verse, which teaches us about serving only one master and making sure that master is God!**

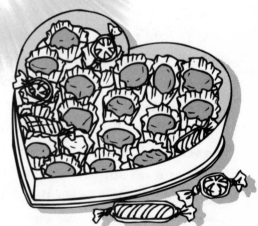

SUPER SCRIPTURE

Before class, write the words to the song "When I Work" from this activity on a sheet of newsprint. Attach the paper to the wall or a door so kids can read the words as they sing. If you don't have the large heart puzzle from last week, cut out another large heart and on it write the Mighty Memory Verse.

Point to the heart puzzle from last week and invite volunteers to repeat the Mighty Memory Verse that's written on the heart. If there's time, carefully take the heart puzzle apart, then have several trios of kids take turns reassembling the puzzle on the floor before finally taping it to the wall or door for next week. If you have older kids, introduce and discuss the extra challenge verse (Galatians 5:13b) at this time.

Say: **This verse tells us how we should serve the Lord. The verse says that whatever work we do, we're to do it with all our hearts for God—not for the approval of other people. In other words, everything we do, we do for God!** Ask:

★ **What are things we can do for God with all our hearts?**

★ **Why does God want us to work with all our hearts?**

★ **Why should we work for God instead of the approval of others?**

Say: **It feels great when we give to God with our whole hearts, because God deserves the best from us! And whether we work, help, serve, pray, play, or sing, the Bible tells us to do it with all our hearts for God. And do you know the best part? God helps us find ways to serve others and to serve him, too. Singing is a fun way to serve the Lord, so let's learn a lively new song about working and serving God with love.**

Sing the following song to the tune of "This Old Man." Substitute words such as *serve, pray, sing, clap,* and *hop* for *work* in subsequent verses. Encourage kids to invent motions to go along with each verse. For example, use raking or shoveling motions for "when I work," and kneel as if praying for "when I pray."

WHEN I WORK

When I work, it's for you,
In the day and nighttime, too.
I will work with love my whole life through;
I will work for only you!

When you finish singing, say: **Wow! That song makes me feel like serving God right now! One of the verses in our song said, "When I pray, it's for you." Prayer is a good way to serve God. Let's share a prayer and a promise as we thank God for his love in helping us serve others and himself.**

A POWERFUL PROMISE

Before class, make a sample hand-to-hand pattern from construction paper. Fold a sheet of construction paper in half, and place your left hand on the paper next to the fold. Trace your hand, leaving the side of it on the fold, then cut out the paper hand. When it's opened, you'll have two hands connected at the sides. Write your name on one hand and the words "I will serve God" on the other. Gather kids and hand each a sheet of colorful construction paper. Hold up the connected hands you made earlier and say: **Let's make helping hands like these to remind us of how we serve God and others.** Show kids how to trace and cut out paper hands, but don't write on the hands yet.

Say: **These hands remind us of today's lesson and all we've learned about serving God and others. We've learned today that when we serve others, we're really serving God, too. We've discovered that God helps us find good ways to serve. And we reviewed the Mighty Memory Verse, which tells us how we're to serve. Colossians 3:23 says** (pause and encourage kids to repeat the verse with you), **"Whatever you do, work at it with all your heart, as working for the Lord, not for men."**

We've learned that one way to serve God is through prayer. When we close our paper hands, they look like prayer hands. Close your prayer hands now and let's share a prayer thanking God for his loving help. Pray: **Dear Lord, we thank you so much for the opportunity to serve you and others in many ways. Please help us find new ways to touch others' lives and serve them with your love and kindness. Amen.**

Say: **God promises to help us find ways to serve others and him. Let's make a promise of our own to God. We can promise to serve God by serving one person each day this week. Think for a moment of people you can serve. Are they at church? at home? at school? in your neighborhood?** Pause, then continue: **Let's write our promises on our helping hands.** Help kids write "I will serve God" on one of their paper hands, then sign their names on the other hands. Say: **Hang your helping hands in a place where you'll see them often as reminders of your promise to serve one person a day for God! Now let's end our time together serving God with the "When I Work" song we learned earlier.** (See page 25.)

Then close with this responsive good-bye:

Leader: **May you serve God and others.**

Children: **And also you!**

Distribute the Power Page! take-home papers as kids are leaving. Thank children for coming and encourage them to keep their promises to God this week.

POWER PAGE!

SERVICE CENTER

See if you can serve in each of these ways during the next week. When you finish one, color in the heart.

♡ Set the table, and clear it, too!

♡ Take a neighbor a special treat.

♡ Empty the wastebaskets.

♡ Tell a friend you care for him.

♡ Write a poem for a teacher.

♡ Express your love to God.

♡ Give someone a hug.

Who Do We Serve?

Use your NIV Bible to fill in the letters to the verses. Then write the letters that match the numbers in the spaces below to discover who we serve.

Galatians 5:13: _ _ _ _ _ _ _
                    5   7

_ _ _ _ _ _ _ _ _ _ .
     2   4

John 12:26: _ _ _ _ _ _ _
               1

_ _ _ _ _ _ _ _ _
     6   3   9

_ _ _ _ _ _ _ .
8

_ _ _ _ _ _ _ _ _ _ _ _
1 2 3 4 1 3 5 3 6 7 3

_ _ _ _ _ _ , _ _
8 9 2 3 6 5   1 3

_ _ _ _ _ G _ D !
5 3 6 7 3   8

Fill-'em-In

Use Colossians 3:23 to fit the missing words into the puzzle.

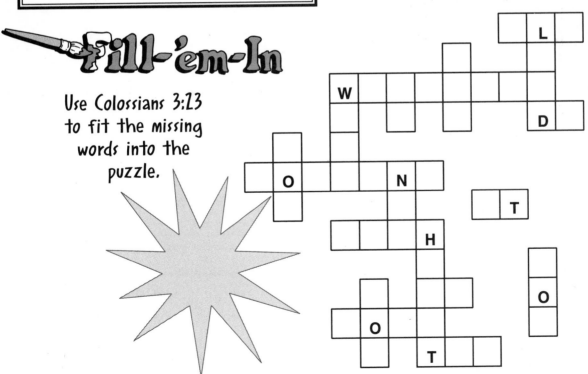

Jesus miracles

TAUGHT BY JESUS

Jesus taught us the value of serving.

Mark 1:9-11
John 2:1-9; 13:3-5, 14, 15

SESSION SUPPLIES

★ Bibles

★ 8-inch squares of paper

★ a pitcher of water

★ markers, glue, and tape

★ glitter glue and sequins

★ self-adhesive bows and newsprint

★ photocopies of the heart-shaped card (page 34)

★ photocopies of the Whiz Quiz (page 36) and the Power Page! (page 35)

MIGHTY MEMORY VERSE

Whatever you do, work at it with all your heart, as working for the Lord, not for men. Colossians 3:23
(For older kids, add in Galatians 5:13b: "Serve one another in love.")

SESSION OBJECTIVES

During this session, children will

★ learn how Jesus served others

★ realize we can imitate Jesus' examples of serving

★ discover that serving demonstrates our love

★ understand that serving means putting others first

BIBLE BACKGROUND

How many of you have watched Julia Child work wonders in the kitchen? Mmm, you can almost taste those tantalizing delights right over the airwaves! Or have you ever painted along with Bob Ross and cheerfully decided where to put your "happy little cloud"? Television is full of demonstration-type shows that instruct us in everything from cooking and sewing to painting and home repair. Why are demonstration shows like this so popular? Because they're effective at teaching people! Learning by example, then imitating that process or action greatly increases our chances of learning and retention. Learning biblical truths and concepts is no different, which is why Jesus spent his entire life giving us examples through which we can learn.

Through studying Jesus' examples of serving God and others, we come away understanding what service is and how it can draw us closer to God while freely giving of ourselves to others. If we strive to imitate even a small fraction of what Jesus taught, then we're well on the way to living as God's instruments of love in action!

Kids are forever shouting, "Show me!" when they see something they'd like to learn. Build upon this natural tendency for imitation by presenting powerful examples of Jesus' service and love in this lesson. Kids will enjoy seeing why examples are powerful teaching tools, then looking for ways to imitate Jesus' selfless love and kindness in their own lives.

POWER FOCUS

Before class, practice folding paper cups so you can direct kids as they fold their own cups. Use 8-inch squares of paper to fold the cups.

As kids arrive, greet them warmly and hand each child a square of paper. Silently hold up your paper until you have kids' attention. Then slowly begin to fold your paper. Stop after each step and motion for kids to imitate your folding steps. Repeat a step if some kids are having problems or motion and smile at another child to help. Don't open the tops of the paper cups.

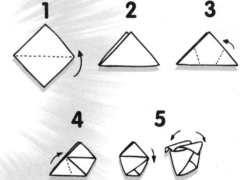

When the cups are folded (kids won't realize they're cups yet, so don't reveal your neat secret), say: **Wow! You were all very good at following and learning by example!** Ask:

★ **How can we learn by imitating other people's examples?**

★ **Why is learning by example good?**

★ **How can we learn by following Jesus' examples of helping, serving, teaching, and being kind to others?**

Say: **Learning by someone else's example is a powerful way to learn because we see that behavior in action! When we read about the examples Jesus gave of serving others or helping them, we not only learn what we can do to serve and help others, we also learn a lot about Jesus!**

Today, we'll be taking a closer look at how Jesus served God and others in his life. We'll discover that serving tells a lot about the person doing the serving. And we'll work on our Mighty Memory Verse that teaches us how we should serve God.

Let's listen to a few great Bible stories about how Jesus served God and others in different ways. Each of these ways involves water, and you can help tell the stories, but first we'll need something to put water in. Open your folded papers like this and see what you find!

Demonstrate how to open the top of the folded paper to make a cup. These cups will hold water for a short time and can be used in the next activity.

Say: **Paper cups! What super story-helpers! Now let's discover how Jesus served up some great examples of serving others!**

THE MIGHTY MESSAGE

Place the water pitcher beside you. Have kids sit around you and hold their paper cups. Say: **One of the best ways to learn something is by someone else's example. Jesus set many examples for us in the Bible, and we learn so much from each one. Let's learn about three times Jesus set powerful examples of serving God, his friends and family, his disciples, and us. As you listen and participate, see if you can decide who Jesus is serving in each example. But first, you need a bit of water to help tell each of the stories.**

Pour a small amount of water in each cup and proceed with the Bible stories as kids follow your directions for using the water.

Say: **Our first story comes from Mark 1. Listen as I read these verses.** Read aloud Mark 1:9-11, then have kids dip their fingers in and out of the water to represent Jesus' baptism. Next, say: **Do you think you know who Jesus was serving? I'll ask you to tell me in a minute. But now let's hear our second story of how Jesus served others. It's found in John 2. See if you can guess who Jesus served now!**

Read aloud John 2:1-7, then pause to have kids sip the water "from the well." Continue reading verses 8 and 9a. Say: **Wow! That was Jesus' first miracle at the wedding in the town of Cana. Do you think you know who Jesus served in that example? Don't tell us yet, because we have one more story to hear. See if you can figure out who Jesus served this time!**

Read aloud John 13:3-5, then pause to let kids dab a bit of water on a friend's hands or feet. Then continue reading verses 14 and 15. Say: **What a powerful example of serving that was! Jesus taught us so much about being kind to others and serving them with loving hearts and spirits! Now let's see if you know who Jesus served in each example!** Have kids finish sipping their water or pour it back into the pitcher. Then ask:

★ **Who was Jesus serving when he was baptized? How did he serve?** (Lead kids to tell that Jesus was serving God.)

★ **Who was Jesus serving when he changed the water to wine? How did he serve them?** (Guide kids to realize that Jesus was serving his mother, his friends, and God.)

★ **Who was Jesus serving when he washed the feet of his disciples? How did he serve them?** (Help kids realize that Jesus was serving his disciples, God, and us as well!)

★ **How are these examples of serving also good examples of Jesus' love?**

★ **In what ways can we imitate Jesus' examples of serving God and others?**

Say: **Jesus had so much love that he always put other people first. He was very unselfish, which is why he could serve so powerfully! Serving means we put other people and God before us. In other words, we can't be selfish when we serve others!** Ask:

★ **In what ways can serving others help us feel good inside? draw us closer to God? show others our love?**

★ **How can you serve God this week? How can you serve another person this week?**

Say: **Jesus spent his whole life serving others and putting them ahead of himself. And best of all, Jesus showed us how to put God very first in our lives! We learn about unselfish love and serving from Jesus' examples of serving others. Let's put unselfish serving into practice right now by finishing our Sweet Service Candy Boxes so they're ready to make others smile with love!**

Set the paper cups aside for now. You'll use them later in the lesson.

THE MESSAGE IN MOTION

Before class, photocopy the heart card from page 34. Kids will be cutting out the cards, coloring them, and embellishing them with glitter, sequins, and markers. You'll need one card for each child plus a card for every three kids. Be sure you've decided to whom you'll present your gift boxes.

Place the cards, markers, glue, glitter glue, and sequins on a table. Have kids get into their project groups and gather the Sweet Service Candy Boxes they've been working on for the past two weeks. Hand each child a heart card and each group an additional card. Invite kids to cut out the cards and use the craft items to embellish them. The group cards will be taped to the tops of the candy boxes, and the individual cards will be used later in the Powerful Promise. Add self-adhesive bows to the box tops.

As kids work, read the two Scripture verses on the heart-shaped cards aloud and discuss what each verse means. Remind kids that when we serve others, we're really serving God, too!

When the boxes are complete and the cards attached, say: **You worked so hard on your sweet service projects!** Ask:

★ **How does it feel to complete a service project that will bring joy to others?**

★ **How does it feel to know you've also served God with your work?**

★ **In what ways did you put love and caring into these sweet boxes?**

Say: **Serving others takes a lot of unselfish love, and it's a wonderful way to show others God's love, too! We can give our Sweet Service Candy Boxes away to the people we've chosen as secret surprises! The Bible tells us that when we serve others and do kind things for them, we can do so in secret—and it's so much fun that way! Matthew 6:3 and 4 says, "Do not let your left hand know what your right hand is doing, so that your giving may be done in secret." But God knows our hearts, and he gets joy from watching us give in secret to others!**

If kids can secretly deliver the boxes, that would be wonderful. Otherwise, assure kids that you'll deliver their service projects in secret. Say: **Now let's review our Mighty Memory Verse as we learn more about working for God with all our hearts.** Set aside the cards kids made until later.

SUPER SCRIPTURE

Before class, draw the Scripture map on page 33 on newsprint and attach it to a wall or door for kids to see. Make sure the large heart puzzle is still usable. If it's torn or lost, cut a new heart from poster board and write the words to Colossians 3:23 on the heart. Then cut the paper heart into six puzzle pieces.

Have kids form two groups. Place the tape and puzzle pieces from the heart on the floor in front of a wall or door. Say: **In this review game, I'll ask one volunteer from each group to repeat the Mighty Memory Verse. If she can say the verse with only one help, that team gets to tape a piece of the puzzle to the wall. Then the other team will have a chance to repeat the verse. If you need help, ask one person from your team to assist you. We'll see if we can get the puzzle assembled on the first try! But first, let's repeat the verse three times together. Practicing God's Word often helps us learn and remember it—and makes it easier to use God's Word in our lives!**

Repeat the verse three times in unison, then begin the review game. Assemble and reassemble the puzzle until everyone has had a chance to repeat the verse.

Say: **When we want to learn how to get someplace, we use a map. When we want to learn Scripture verses, a Scripture map can be a great help!** Show kids the Scripture map on the wall or door. Explain how the map works as you repeat portions of the verse along each stop. Then invite kids to use a ruler or fin-

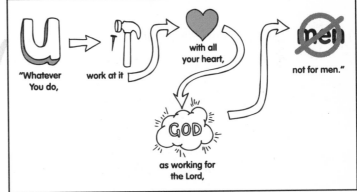

gers as pointers on the map while another child repeats the verse. The concrete visual and the words will help lock away this verse in hearts and minds!

After several repetitions, hand out the paper cups made earlier and let kids use markers to draw the Scripture map on their cups to take home for practicing the verse.

Say: **God promises to help us map out ways to serve him and others. And we can promise God to be willing servants! Let's share a prayer and a promise.**

A POWERFUL PROMISE

Have kids sit in a circle holding the cards they made earlier. Say: **We've been learning so much about the importance and value of serving God and others. Today we discovered that serving others takes an unselfish attitude and is a way to demonstrate our love and kindness. We learned that Jesus served God and others throughout his entire life and that we** can learn from his examples. And we reviewed the **Mighty Memory Verse that says** (pause and encourage kids to repeat the verse with you), **"Whatever you do, work at it with all your heart, as working for the Lord, not for men."**

Hold up the Bible and say: **Serving others is one of the most important lessons we can learn from Jesus. As we pass the Bible around our circle, let's make our own special promises. We can say, "I want to serve you and others, God."** Pass the Bible until everyone has had a chance to make a promise.

Say: **Take your cards with you and present your card to someone in the next week as a way of serving. It will lovingly remind that person to be on the lookout for ways to serve God and others, too!**

Before kids leave, allow five or ten minutes to complete the Whiz Quiz from page 36. If you run out of time, be sure to do this page first thing next week. The Whiz Quiz is an invaluable tool that allows kids, teachers, and parents to see what kids have learned in the previous three weeks.

If there's time, sing the lively song you learned last week to the tune of "This Old Man." (See page 25 if you've forgotten the words.)

End with this responsive good-bye:

Leader: **May God's love help you serve!**

Children: **And also you!**

Distribute the Power Page! take-home papers as children are leaving. Thank kids for coming and encourage them to keep their promises to God this week.

Candy is dandy, but SERVING is sweeter!

Serve one another in love. (Galatians 5:13)

Serve wholeheartedly, as if you were serving the Lord, not men. (Ephesians 6:7)

POWER PAGE!

MIGHTY MATCH-UPS

Look up and read the verses on the left that tell how Jesus served God and others. Then draw lines to the ways Jesus served on the right.

John 2:1-11   Jesus served God by being baptized.

John 13:3-5   Jesus served his friends at the wedding at Cana.

Mark 1:9-11   Jesus served his disciples and taught us about serving others.

Care to Share?

Copy this coupon onto five index cards, then hand them to five friends, family members, or neighbors to redeem. Be sure to give service with a smile!

CARE COUPON

Good for your choice of 1 free ...

★ hug   ★ picture   ★ song

★ chore   ★ errand   ★ poem

Jesus served me and you ...

Jesus served so we can, too!

LETTER BEFORE

Write the letter that comes <u>before</u> the letter under each space. Hint: Use Colossians 3:23 to help you!

__ __ __ __ __ __ __   __ __ __   __ __ ,   __ __ __ __   __ __   __ __   __ __ __ __

X I B U F W F S   Z P V   E P   X P S L   B U   J U   X J U I

__ __ __   __ __ __ __   __ __ __ __ ,   __ __   __ __ __ __ __ __ __   __ __ __

B M M   Z P V S   I F B S U   B T   X P S L J O H   G P S

__ __ __   __ __ __ __ ,   __ __ __   __ __ __   __ __ __ .

U I F   M P S E   O P U   G P S   N F O

WHIZ QUIZ

Color in YES or NO to answer each question.

✳ Serving others doesn't help them.   (YES) (NO)

✳ When we serve others, we serve God.   (YES) (NO)

✳ Even Jesus served God.   (YES) (NO)

✳ God doesn't care if we serve others or not.   (YES) (NO)

✳ Jesus taught us to serve by his examples.   (YES) (NO)

✳ Learning God's Word and praying are ways to serve.   (YES) (NO)

Scripture Swirl

Use the words below to fill
in the missing words to the
MIGHTY MEMORY VERSE.

you	with
work	at
it	as
all	your
heart	for
Lord	the
working	Colossians
3	men
not	do
for	23

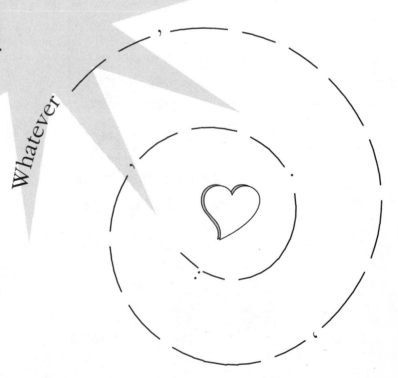

Whatever

SERVANT LEADERS IN THE OLD TESTAMENT

And we know that in all
things God works for the
good of those who love him,
who have been called according
to his purpose.
Romans 8:28

IN MOSES' FOOTSTEPS

God calls us to be his leaders.

Exodus 3:1-12;
Joshua 1:6-9

SESSION SUPPLIES

★ Bibles
★ large, bouncy ball
★ photocopies of the footprint on page 126
★ black construction paper
★ scissors and tape
★ pairs of old tennis shoes
★ glitter glue, plastic jewels, and sequins
★ potting soil and seeds
★ white crayons and markers
★ newsprint and newspaper
★ photocopies of the Power Page! (page 45)

MIGHTY MEMORY VERSE

And we know that in all things God works for the good of those who love him, who have been called according to his purpose. Romans 8:28

SESSION OBJECTIVES

During this session, children will
★ realize that God calls us to be his leaders
★ understand that good leaders also serve
★ identify character qualities of leaders
★ recognize their own gifts of leadership

BIBLE BACKGROUND

Remember the childhood favorite, *The Little Red Hen?* Poor Red lived with friends who were more than willing to gobble down an entire cake but balked when called upon to help bake it. Many of us find ourselves in similar spots when we're called by God to lead and serve. We're willing, we're able, but when we're called, we balk. Hesitancy comes from many sources: fear, laziness, insecurities, or self doubt, as in Moses' case. When God called upon Moses at the burning bush, Moses' first response was, "Here I am, Lord." Moses showed his willingness to approach God. But when God revealed his plan for Moses, Moses hesitated: "I can't." "Who am I to do this?" "Why me?" But God answered Moses' doubts with five simple words that are the answer to our own fears of serving God as well: "I will be with you!"

Kids look up to leaders and long for the same qualities they see displayed by these men and women: bravery, faith, trust, and obedience. Even though they are young, kids realize that these important qualities enable leaders to accomplish great things. Help kids to identify these qualities in their own lives as you discover how Moses went from an "I can't" kind of guy to a powerful leader for the Lord.

POWER focus

Before class, you'll need to clear a play area if you're playing this game indoors. If you have room to toss the ball, that's fine. If space is at a premium, simply bounce the ball hard and let kids run to catch the ball on the bounce instead of the toss.

Gather kids in a circle and stand in the center holding a playground ball or large ball that bounces easily. Say: **I have a fun game to start us off today! It's called Call-Ball, and it's a lively game of listening and responding. I'll toss the ball in the air and call out someone's name. If it's your name that is called, you must run in and catch the ball before it touches the ground. If you catch the ball in time, you may call the next name. If the ball touches the floor, I'll call another name and you can go back to the circle to keep playing until your name is called again.**

Continue bouncing or tossing the ball and calling names until everyone has successfully caught the ball and had a chance to toss or bounce it and call out another child's name. Then have kids sit in a circle and ask:

★ **What did you do when your name was called?**

★ **Why did you hop into action? What would have happened if you had not moved?**

★ **How is this game like when God calls us to do something for him or for someone else?**

Say: **This game was a game of reaction. When your name was called, you jumped into action and got the job done! If you'd have kept sitting, you never would have accomplished the goal of catching the ball.**

Our lesson today is all about how God calls us into action and how we want to jump to it when God calls us to be his leaders! We'll learn

about the qualities leaders must have and how all good leaders also serve others. And we'll begin a new Mighty Memory Verse that teaches us how things work out when we serve as God's leaders!

Right now, let's listen to a Bible story about an Old Testament leader named Moses, who jumped into action when God called his name to lead. Set the ball aside until later.

THE **MIGHTY** MESSAGE

Before class, enlarge the footprint on page 126 so it's about half again the size of a child's footprint. Cut out a set of black construction-paper footprints for each child plus one extra set. (You'll be using pairs of footprints for the next five lessons as well, so you may wish to cut out seven more pairs to be prepared! You'll need three pairs for lesson 6.)

Hand each child a set of footprints and tape them on the kids' shoes. Ask the kids to explain what it means to "walk in someone else's shoes." Help the children understand that this means seeing how another person feels, thinks, and acts in order to gain understanding of why that person does what he does.

Say: **These simple props will help you tell the story of how Moses was called into action by God. Walk carefully in Moses' footsteps as we tell the story!** Retell the following story from Exodus 3:1-12 as you lead kids in the accompanying motions.

Say: **Moses loved God and obeyed him all the time. Moses prayed** (kneel and pray) **and talked to God every day and followed wherever God would lead him.** (Walk to one side of the room.) **One day, Moses was tending a flock of sheep by Mount Horeb when he noticed a strange sight.** (Point to the other side of the room.) **An angel of the Lord appeared to Moses in flames of fire coming from inside a bush! Moses was amazed and wanted a closer look at a bush that was on fire but didn't burn up. So Moses came closer.** (Walk slowly across the room.)

When Moses was near the bush, God called to him. "Moses! Moses!" called God. And Moses said, "Here I am." God told Moses not to come any closer, but to remove his sandals, for he was on holy ground. (Have

POWER POINTERS

Give kids opportunities to display leadership in your classroom. Encourage kids to lead prayers, Bible readings, and even simple devotions and stories whenever possible.

kids carefully untape the footprints and set them to one side.) **God told Moses he was the God of his ancestors, the God of Abraham, Isaac, and Jacob. What do you think Moses did then?** Pause for responses. Then continue: **Moses hid his face, for he was very afraid!** (Have kids kneel and hide their faces.)

God told Moses he wanted Moses to become his leader and help the Israelite people, who were being kept as slaves in Egypt. But Moses didn't think he could be a leader for God. Moses said, "Who am I to go and save the Israelites?" But God assured Moses that he would be with Moses and help him all the way. So Moses put on his sandals and went to obey God! (Have kids re-tape the footprints to their shoes.)

Lead kids back to the other side of the room chanting, "I will go and serve you, God!" Then have kids sit in a group and ask:

★ **What did Moses do when God called his name?**

★ **Why do you think Moses was afraid he couldn't do the job? Have you ever felt that way?**

★ **How does it help knowing that God is with us to help us serve?**

★ **What do you think might have happened if Moses hadn't obeyed God and become his leader?**

★ **What can we learn from Moses about being good leaders for God?**

Say: **Moses came when God called and obeyed when God wanted him to serve as a leader. Even though Moses felt unsure of himself, he obeyed and trusted God. And we can learn, as Moses did, that God helps us lead even when we're unsure or afraid!** Ask:

★ **What leadership qualities did Moses have?** (Lead kids to suggest traits such as trust, faith, love, courage, obedience, and listening to God.)

Read Joshua 1:6-9, then ask:

★ **What qualities can we develop to become strong leaders for God?**

Write Moses' name on one of the footsteps and qualities such as trust, faith, and obedience on the other. Tape the footsteps to the wall or a door. You'll add footsteps for each Bible character you learn about for the next five weeks.

Have kids use white crayons to list on one of their footsteps qualities they'd like to have as leaders. Then set the pairs of footsteps aside until later.

Say: **God helps us have these qualities in our lives when we know, love, and follow him! And because we** can follow in the footsteps of Bible heroes such as Moses, we have great examples to follow! Let's start a new service project today as we learn more about being in the footsteps of a leader!

THE MESSAGE IN MOTION

Before class, collect enough pairs of old tennis shoes so each child has one shoe. You'll be using these as planters, so it doesn't matter if there are holes, missing laces, stains, or other old areas on the shoes. You will also need to collect colorful permanent markers and sparkly craft items such as plastic jewels, sequins, and glitter glue.

Finally, you will need a variety of quick-sprouting seeds such as peas, beans, marigolds, and radishes. You will want to prepare in advance a shoe planter for the kids to see as a sample, as well as having one you'll use during the next couple of weeks in class.

Cover a table with newspaper and set out the craft items, glue, potting soil, and seeds. Hand each child an old tennis shoe and say: **We've been learning about what it's like to be in the footsteps of a leader such as Moses. For our three-week service project, we'll be collecting foot gear to donate. But today, we're going to make planters to remind us how we need to grow leadership qualities in our lives so we can follow in the footsteps of leaders such as Moses.**

Have kids decorate the sides of the shoes with sparkly sequins, plastic jewels, and glitter glue. Then help kids write "Footsteps of God's leader" on one side of their shoes. When the decorating is complete, have kids fill the shoes with potting soil, then plant several seeds in the soil. Spritz the soil with water, then tell kids to set their mini gardens in a sunny spot at home and to keep them moist until the plants sprout. Keep one mini garden in class to watch the plants grow as your donations grow!

Say: **While we wait for the plants in the planters to sprout and grow, let's be collecting gently worn shoes and slippers, new socks, and other types of footwear that we can give to a local clothing bank. Next week, we'll decorate collection boxes to set around the church and community so others have a chance to donate items, too. We'll see how many pairs of footwear we can collect before our plants are three inches tall!**

Ask friends and family to donate footwear, then bring in any donations next week. Take your planters home and remember that we can walk in the footsteps of God's leaders when we grow qualities like trust, faith, courage, and obedience in our lives. Now let's learn a new Mighty Memory Verse as we learn even more about being the Lord's leaders!

SUPER SCRIPTURE

Before class, draw the Scripture map from this activity on newsprint and tape it to a wall or door so kids can see and copy it later.

Gather kids and help them find Romans 8:28 in their Bibles. Read the verse aloud two times, then break the verse into several sections and have kids echo the portions after you.

Turn kids' attention to the Scripture map. Say: **We've used a Scripture map before to help us learn God's Word. Let's look at each part of the map and repeat the words that accompany the pictures.**
Point to each picture and read the accompanying words as you wind your way around the Scripture map. Then invite pairs of kids to come to the map. Have one partner point to the pictures while the other partner reads the words.

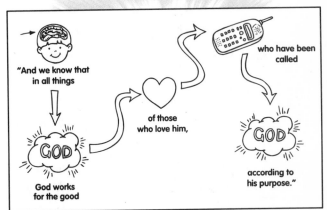

Say: **What an important verse! Just think, even when we think things aren't going well, they work out for the best when we love God and follow him! Let's compare how things worked out for Moses using this verse.**

★ **"And we know that in all things God works for the good of those who love him"—Did Moses love God? How do we know that?**

★ **"Who have been called"—Did God call Moses? How did Moses respond?**

★ **"According to his purpose"—Did everything work out according to God's purpose? How did Moses fit into God's purpose?**

Repeat the verse two more times in unison. Then say: **Moses wasn't sure things would work out when God called him to be a leader. But Moses trusted God and obeyed him, and everything worked out good and according to God's purpose! I'm so glad that God will help us be his leaders, too! We can thank God in prayer for his help and ask him to**

help us develop strong leadership qualities to serve him according to his purpose! Keep the Scripture map to use in next week's lesson.

A POWERFUL PROMISE

Have kids sit in a circle and hold their pairs of paper footprints. Ask for a moment of silence, then say: **We've learned today that God calls us to be his faithful leaders and that we have to be ready to go when we're called. We also discovered that God's leaders have qualities such as trust, faith, and obedience.** Have kids read the qualities they listed on their paper footsteps.

Continue: **And we began learning a new Mighty Memory Verse that teaches us that all things work for good when we love God. Romans 8:28 says** (pause and encourage kids to repeat the verse with you), **"And we know that in all things God works for the good of those who love him, who have been called according to his purpose."**

Hold up the Bible and say: **God promises to be with us all the time and to help us become strong leaders, if we love and trust him! Let's make a promise of our own to God. We can commit to growing the qualities we listed on our footsteps and to look for ways to use those qualities when God calls upon us. As we pass the Bible around our circle, we can say, "I want to grow leadership qualities for you, God."** Pass the Bible until everyone has had a chance to make a promise.

End with a prayer thanking God for guiding us as his leaders and asking for God's help in growing leadership qualities like Moses' in our lives.

Pass the white crayon around the circle and have everyone sign her name on the other paper footstep. As kids sign their names, say: **Signing our names is a way to tell God we're serious about wanting to have leadership qualities in our lives. Hang your footsteps someplace at home where you can see them often and be reminded of the qualities we want in our lives to be good leaders for the Lord.**

End with this responsive good-bye:

Leader: **May you be a strong leader for God.**

Children: **And also you!**

Distribute the Power Page! take-home papers as kids are leaving. Thank children for coming and encourage them to keep their promises to God this week. Remind kids to bring in any shoes, slippers, new socks, or other footwear next week for the service project.

POWER PAGE!

QUALITIES COUNT!

Fill in the missing words. The circled letters will tell what leaders do for God and others.

1. God wants leaders to _____ him.

T _ _ O _

2. When we do what we're told, we ____.

O _ O _

3. Leaders don't lie— tell the _____.

T O _ _ _

4. Leaders are _____ and courageous.

B _ _ O _

5. Leaders ____ God!

L _ _ O

POWER CHALLENGE!

See if you can organize the kids in your class or neighborhood to hold a "bucket brigade" car wash. You'll need:

* sponges and rags
* bubble bath
   (it's gentle on cars)
* buckets of water

Wet the cars, then wash them with soapy water. Give the cars a final rinse and they'll shine like new! For a fun touch, put a Scripture card under the windshield wipers. (Be sure to ask permission to give cars a bath!)

LOST LETTERS

The vowels in Romans 8:28 are missing. See if you can replace each one to finish the verse.

__nd w__ kn__w th__t __n __ll th__ngs G__d w__rks f__r th__ g__ __d __f th__se wh__ l__ve h__m, wh__ h__ve b__ __n c__ll__d __cc__rd__ng t__ h__s p__rp__s__ .

LEADING LADY: DEBORAH!

To lead others, we must follow God.

Judges 4:4-16
5:1-3, 9-12, 31

SESSION SUPPLIES

★ Bibles
★ a pair of black construction-paper footprints
★ paper, glue, tape, and a white crayon
★ scissors and markers
★ newsprint and gift wrap
★ three large boxes
★ aluminum foil and brass paper fasteners
★ photocopies of the Courage Cards (page 123)
★ photocopies of the Power Page! (page 53)

MIGHTY MEMORY VERSE

And we know that in all things God works for the good of those who love him, who have been called according to his purpose. Romans 8:28

(For older kids, add in John 12:26: "Whoever serves me must follow me; and where I am, my servant also will be. My Father will honor the one who serves me.")

SESSION OBJECTIVES

During this session, children will
★ discover that God can call anyone to lead
★ realize that being a leader takes courage
★ identify more qualities of God's leaders
★ learn that leading requires following God

BIBLE BACKGROUND

Congratulations, and God bless you! The fact that you are reading this opening introduction is delightful proof that you're already a servant leader for God and his children! Wouldn't it be wonderful if more people were so willing to serve with their time and talents? But many would-be servants and could-be leaders complain of not enough time, too many previous commitments, and a host of other reasons why they're unable to step forward when God calls. Deborah faced a similar challenge when General Barak refused to step forward for God and lead the Israelite army to victory. But Deborah trusted God and was ready and willing to lead. And lead she did! The Israelites marched to victory, and Deborah marched into our hearts as the woman with strength enough to serve heroically—even in the heat of battle!

Kids love stories with unlikely heroes winning victories. Who would expect a woman to rise up and lead God's army to such a victory? Give kids pause to contemplate the possibility of God using them in powerful ways. After all, God can and does choose anyone he wants to be his leaders!

POWER FOCUS

Before class, photocopy and cut out the Courage Cards from page 123.

Seat kids in a circle and invite them to tell about times they had to have courage or bravery. Encourage them to tell how they felt being brave or even what it was like not to feel so brave and to ask for someone's help. Then say: **It's hard to be brave when we're not confident we can do a job right or when we have to face someone or something we might be unsure of. Let's play a quick game of Courage Cards to see how brave you might be in different situations. I'll choose a volunteer to come read a card silently. Then he can follow the directions on the card or ask for help by letting someone else try.**

Call on volunteers to read cards and follow directions. Don't force anyone to take a card, but encourage children to do so. Remind kids that they can ask for someone's help if they feel they can't follow a direction.

When the cards are used up and most kids have had a chance to follow directions, ask:

★ **What made you decide whether to follow the directions or ask someone else to follow them?**

★ **How did you feel if you decided not to follow a direction?**

★ **How are bravery and trust related? courage and faith?**

Say: **It's not always easy to follow directions, is it? But when those directions are from God, we want to have the courage to follow them no matter what! Today we'll be learning that, to be a good leader, we have to be a courageous follower! We'll explore how God can call anyone to lead and learn that we have to rely on God to help us follow through. We'll also work on our Mighty Memory Verse that teaches us how to trust God's purpose in everything. But first let's hear an exciting Bible story about one of God's brave warrior leaders. You'll find it very surprising!**

THE **MIGHTY** MESSAGE

Before class, you may wish to find different pictures of Hebrew warriors from Bible reference books or storybooks. Don't use a picture of Deborah, since part of the surprise in this activity is the fact that Deborah was a woman leader. You'll also need a white crayon and a pair of black construction-paper footprints cut out last week. (See page 40.)

Hand each child a sheet of paper and invite kids to draw pictures of what they think a leader of the nation of Israel might have looked like. Remind kids that Israel was surrounded by many enemies at that time and often had to go to war to defend themselves. If you have found pictures, show them to the kids. Encourage kids to use bits of foil or brass paper fasteners to embellish their pictures. As they work, explain that early soldiers often wore breastplates made of thick leather and carried shields that had wooden frames with thick leather stretched across them. Point out that most warriors carried weapons, which included swords, axes, and knives, and that many soldiers wore greaves, leather protectors strapped around their lower legs.

Allow five minutes for kids to finish the pictures, then have children hold up their artwork.

Say: **My, these are wonderful warrior leaders; they look so fierce! I'm sure they'd be strong enough to lead God's army into any battle. But these warriors don't quite fit the description of the leader in our Bible story today. As I tell the story, see if you can figure out what this leader of God's people was like!**

In Old Testament days, the Canaanites were mean people who didn't love God. They would attack God's people and steal their crops and herds. Now Deborah was a prophetess and a judge for God's people who loved and trusted God very much. Deborah called the general of the Israelite army, whose name was Barak. Deborah told Barak that God was ordering him to take ten thousand soldiers and go to fight the Canaanites. But Barak was afraid and said, "I will go only if you come and lead us!"

Deborah trusted God and knew God had promised his people the victory. So Deborah went with Barak and the others into battle. Did they

POWER POINTERS

Help kids brainstorm to name other women of the Bible who were servant leaders and helped accomplish God's plans. Suggest Mary, Martha, Ruth, Rahab, and Esther as good examples.

win the battle? Yes! The battle belonged to God, and his people won! Lead children in a lively round of applause for Deborah and God's victory. Then ask:

★ **How accurately does your picture portray God's leader in this story?**

★ **Were you surprised to discover God's leader was a woman? Why or why not?**

★ **Why was Deborah a good leader? Was she brave? Explain.**

★ **How did Deborah show God she trusted him? loved him?**

★ **In what ways can being good followers make us good leaders?**

Have kids throw away their pictures, then say: **Just as we threw away our pictures, sometimes we have to throw away our ideas about who God can use as a leader. God doesn't look at whether we're men or women or whether we're big or small or short or tall. God knows the heart of a leader is focused on following him and is full of trust, faith, and bravery! And these were qualities God saw in Deborah!**

Ask a child to write Deborah's name on one of the black footprints and Deborah's leadership qualities on the other footprint. Write words such as *obeyed* or *followed God, trust,* and *courage.* Tape the footprints to the wall above the ones for Moses from last week. You'll add another pair of footprints next week.

Say: **Deborah knew Barak was afraid to follow God, but she wasn't. Deborah showed God her love and trust by following what he told her to do. Those were brave footprints Deborah made going off to war! Let's make some tracks of our own right now as we continue working on the service project we began last week. It will help remind us of walking in the footsteps of God's brave leaders!**

THE MESSAGE IN MOTION

Have kids form three service groups and give each group a large box. Invite kids to use festive gift wrap to decorate the boxes with patterns of shoes or funny socks if possible. You may wish to bring in several pairs of socks to help decorate the boxes.

As kids work, ask the following questions and have kids discuss the answers in their groups:

★ **How does trusting God help us be courageous leaders and followers?**

★ **What leadership qualities do you see in yourself that would make you a good leader for God?**

★ **How do you feel knowing that God can call anyone to be his leader?**

★ **In what ways does serving others show leadership? love for others? love for God?**

When all of the boxes have been decorated, help kids write "Step by Step We Can All Help!" in large letters on one side of the boxes. Explain that the boxes will be placed in the church or at stores in the community to invite others to be servant leaders and help with their donations. Tell kids that the donation boxes will be picked up just before class next week for the finishing touches!

Say: **Being servant leaders is fun and makes everyone feel great! God wants us to serve others, and there are so many ways we can serve! We can be leaders for God by setting good examples of helping others. We can sing songs that encourage others to feel God's love. And we can serve by learning God's Word and putting it to use in our lives. Let's serve God right now by reviewing our Mighty Memory Verse and discovering ways to put that verse into action today!**

SUPER SCRIPTURE

Before class, write the words to the song in this activity on newsprint and tape it to a wall or door for kids to read while singing later. Be sure the Scripture map from last week is still attached to the wall. If you need to make a new map, refer to page 43 for directions.

Gather kids around the Scripture map and challenge pairs of kids to repeat Romans 8:28 in unison. Challenge kids to use the Scripture map only if they feel they need extra help, then see if they can repeat the verse without using the map. If you have older kids, introduce John 12:26 at this time and give kids several chances to repeat the verse with their partners. This is a long extra challenge verse, so you may wish to learn only the first or last part.

Say: **One way to serve God is by learning his Word. Another good way is through song. Let's combine the two as we sing our Mighty Memory**

Verse to God. We'll sing Romans 8:28 to the tune of "Old MacDonald Had a Farm." Here are the words to the song!

Read the words to the Scripture song aloud, then sing the song through two times. As kids sing the words "Faith, trust, solid nerve—we're God's leaders who will serve!" have them march and shout.

And we know that in all things,
God works for the good
Of those who love him and been called
According to his will!
Faith, trust,
Solid nerve—
We're God's leaders who will serve!
And we know that in all things,
God works for the good!

Say: **This is such an important Scripture verse. What do you think it means?** Invite kids to share their thoughts, then say: **God's Word is telling us that when we love God, all things will work out according to his purpose or plans. In other words, we can trust God to work things out when we love him and follow his plans. Yes!** Ask:

★ **How does being obedient help us accomplish God's plans?**

★ **How does being a brave follower help things work out for the good?**

Say: **Last week, we learned what a good leader Moses was. Why, we even checked Moses out against this Scripture verse to see what kind of leader he was! Let's check Deborah out against this verse and see if she was a good leader. I'll repeat portions of Romans 8:28, then ask you a question or two.**

★ **"And we know that in all things God works for the good of those who love him"—Did Deborah love God? How do we know that?**

★ **"Who have been called"—Did God call Deborah? How did she respond?**

★ **"According to his purpose"—Did everything work out according to God's purpose? How did Deborah fit into God's purpose!**

Say: **God promised Deborah that he would deliver the enemy into the hands of the Israelites, and God's people would win the battle. Did it happen as God had planned? Yes! That's because Deborah was a brave leader who helped accomplish things according to God's purpose. And** after the battle, Deborah did something else to show she was a great leader. Let's discover what she did as we get ready to pray. Keep the Scripture map to use next week.

A POWERFUL PROMISE

Gather kids in a circle and say: **When Deborah and the Israelites won the battle with the Canaanites, Deborah knew that the battle had actually been won by God. Deborah had been a courageous leader, but she didn't want to take the credit because she knew God had accomplished his plans through his power and her help. To thank and give God the glory, Deborah sang a song to God. Let's bow our heads in prayerful silence as I read portions of Deborah's powerful victory song to God.** Read aloud Judges 5:1-3, 9-12, and 31. End the reading with a corporate "amen."

Say: **What an exciting time we've had discovering about Deborah, the brave woman who was a servant leader for the Lord! We've learned that God can call anyone to be a leader and will help his leaders be brave and accomplish his will. We've explored more qualities of leadership, such as courage and trust. And we also reviewed the Mighty Memory Verse, which says** (pause) **"And we know that in all things God works for the good of those who love him, who have been called according to his purpose. Romans 8:28."** If you have older kids, repeat the extra challenge verse with them at this time.

Let's make a promise to God today. We can promise to be available when God calls and to follow his lead so his plans are accomplished. Let's pass the Bible around our circle and say, "I will be ready to serve you, Lord." Pass the Bible until everyone has had a chance to make a promise.

Say: **Deborah sang a song to serve God, and so can we! Let's close by singing the song we learned earlier.** Remind kids that the words are on the newsprint if they need help.

End with this responsive good-bye:

Leader: **May you be God's servant leaders.**

Children: **And also you!**

Distribute the Power Page! take-home papers as kids are leaving. Thank children for coming and encourage them to keep their promises to God this week. Remind kids to bring in their shoe, slipper, and sock collections next week for the service project.

POWER PAGE!

DRAW DEBORAH
Then dress her in the full armor of God!

SOLDIER'S ARMOR

Read Ephesians 6:12-17 to discover what pieces are in the full armor of God. Then draw lines to the matching pictures.

feet fitted with the ____ of _____

the _____ of faith

the _____ of the Spirit

the ____ of truth

the ____ of righteousness

the _____ of salvation

Scripture Map
Follow the map and write in the missing words to Romans 8:28 below each picture.

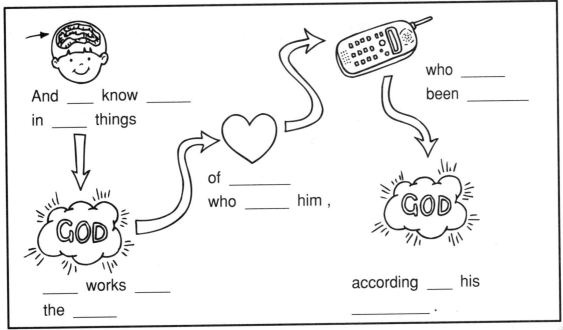

And ___ know _____ in _____ things

GOD

_____ works _____ the _____

of _____ who _____ him ,

who _____ been _____

GOD

according ___ his _____ .

Daniel

A FIERY EXAMPLE

Leaders set good examples for others.

Daniel 3:1-30

Romans 10:15

1 Timothy 4:12

MIGHTY MEMORY VERSE

And we know that in all things God works for the good of those who love him, who have been called according to his purpose. Romans 8:28

(For older kids, add in John 12:26: "Whoever serves me must follow me; and where I am, my servant also will be. My Father will honor the one who serves me.")

SESSION SUPPLIES

★ Bibles

★ one black and one white hat or cap

★ yellow and orange crepe paper

★ scissors and tape

★ markers and crayons

★ three pairs of black construction-paper footprints

★ newsprint and a white crayon

★ colorful satin ribbon

★ photocopies of the gift cards (page 126)

★ photocopies of Romans 8:28 (page 127)

★ photocopies of the Whiz Quiz (page 62) and the Power Page! (page 61)

SESSION OBJECTIVES

During this session, children will

★ learn that setting good examples is a way to serve

★ discover that leaders encourage others

★ realize that leaders are loyal to God

★ express thanks for God's help in setting good examples

BIBLE BACKGROUND

Though many would choose to be known by their words, the truth is, we're known better by our actions! Even the Bible tells us that words of faith are empty unless they are put into motion and use. We learn by example, and we teach others through our own examples of speaking, acting, living, giving, loving—and serving. Imitation is said to be the sincerest form of compliment, but it may also be the most powerful form of servant leadership when we emulate Bible heroes such as the three friends who bravely faced Nebuchadnezzar's fiery furnace. Shadrach, Meshach, and Abednego set powerful examples for the crowds that gathered to worship the king's brazen idol. And when the heat was on, the three friends glowed through their shining example of loyalty, love, and obedience to God! If actions speak louder than words, we can live our lives shouting praises to God through the solid examples we set for others.

Kids need sound examples to model their own lives after. Like chalkboards blank and ready for input, kids need healthy, God-centered role models on which to base their own actions, courage, and strength of character. Use this lesson to help kids see the powerful examples of servant leadership Shadrach, Meshach, and Abednego set for us when they faced their fiery challenge.

POWER FOCUS

Before class collect a black hat or cap and a white one. Baseball caps, cowboy hats, stocking caps, or other headgear is fine.

Gather kids and set the hats beside you. Invite children to tell about times someone tried to coax them into doing something wrong, such as skipping school, stealing something from a store, telling a lie, or cheating on a test. Encourage kids to explain how they "stuck to their guns" and refused or how they felt later, if they gave in.

Then say: **Let's play a quick game of Coax Me! We'll form two groups and switch after each round. One group is the black hats and can choose someone to wear the black hat. The other group is the white hats and can choose someone to wear the white hat. The black hats are to try to convince the white hats to do something that they may not agree with. They can beg, convince, wheedle, and say whatever they need to get the white hats to give in. The white hats must give solid reasons why they won't go along with the black hats' suggestions. We'll see if the white hats are strong and smart enough to keep saying "No!" and to give reasons why they won't give in. Then we'll switch groups.**

Use the following situations to begin the "debates." Encourage both sides to come up with as many solid and logical reasons as they can to either agree or disagree with the situation. After a few moments of debate, see if the white team held their own and wasn't convinced to do the wrong thing. Then switch groups and have the black hats become the white hats and vice versa.

★ *Go ahead—steal that piece of gum!*

★ *Hey! We can skip Sunday school just for today!*

★ *Let's not give our money to the poor. We can buy ice cream instead!*

★ *We can skip our chores and play baseball instead!*

After role-playing the good guys and bad guys, say: **That acting-out game was fun, but it also made us think about our choices and our actions! You all did a good job of saying no and sticking to your guns!** Ask:

★ **Why is it often hard to say no?**

★ **Where do we get the strength to say no and stick to it?**

★ **In what ways does serving God help each of us set a good example of saying no when we need to?**

Say: **It's often hard to do the right thing even when we know that doing the wrong thing will get us into trouble! But when we know, love, and follow God, he helps us do the right things! God helps us set good examples for others by helping us make solid choices and recognizing when we ought to say no.**

Today we'll learn that being a leader for God means setting good examples for others to follow. We'll discover that God helps us do the right things. And we'll also review our Mighty Memory Verse that assures us things will turn out good when we love God. First, let's hear an exciting story about three friends who discovered how God helps us say no and avoid life's hot spots!

POWER POINTERS

Challenge kids to set an example for their families by volunteering to read a Scripture verse from the Bible each night at dinner!

THE **MIGHTY** MESSAGE

Before class, cut the yellow and orange crepe paper into 2-foot lengths. Be sure you have three more pairs of black construction-paper footprints cut out for the three friends in today's Bible story. (Refer to page 40 for the pattern.) You will need to cut a yellow and an orange paper strip for each child. You will also want to write the following rhyming couplet on a sheet of newsprint and place it so the children can read the words.

The heat is on, but we will show
That we serve God—the answer's "No!"

Have kids form a circle and say: **This is such an exciting Bible story!
But to act it out, we need three volunteers to act as Shadrach,
Meshach, and Abednego, the three friends in the story. We also need
someone to play the part of God's heavenly helper.** Choose four volunteers and have the three friends stand in the center of the circle.
Position the heavenly helper outside the circle. Say: **The rest of us
will play different parts and will need these crepe paper strips
to help. Just follow along with my words, and I'll tell you what to do!**

Read the following action story from Daniel 3. At the appropriate times,
have the three friends repeat the rhyming couplet. And when the friends are
tossed into the fiery furnace, have the kids holding the crepe-paper streamers
rustle them around the floor like flames as the three friends and the heavenly
helper walk among the flames.

**Once there was a king named Nebuchadnezzar who didn't know or
love God. The king thought he was very fine—almost a god himself! Bad
King Nebuchadnezzar!** (Have kids shake their fingers.) **King Nebuchadnezzar built a big, huge, monstrously gigantic golden idol. It was ninety
feet high and nine feet wide! Whoa—what an awful thing it was! Then
King Nebuchadnezzar made a law that whenever music played, everyone was to bow down and to worship the golden idol, or they would be
tossed into a fiery furnace of flickering flames! Bad King
Nebuchadnezzar!** (Have kids shake their fingers.)

**There were also three friends living in the king's land. Their names
were Shadrach, Meshach, and Abednego. They loved God and would worship only him! What do you think the friends said when they heard about
the king's new law?** (Have the three friends repeat the rhyming couplet.)

Continue: **The crowd watched and listened to see what would happen.
And the king shouted, "Turn up the heat, toss them in! They won't worship my idol, but I'll surely win! This is the last time I'll ask—will you
bow down?" But the three friends kept saying,** (repeat the rhyming couplet).

Have kids rustle their crepe-paper streamers on the ground as flames. Say:
**Then they tied up the three friends and turned the heat up seven times
hotter than usual! Ouch! The heat was on, but the three friends had faith
in God and kept saying,** (repeat the rhyme). **Then something amazing
happened!** (Send in the child playing the part of the heavenly helper.) **The
king shouted, "We tossed in three, but I see four! How in the world could**

there be one more?" God had sent a heavenly helper to show he would save the three friends. They were all walking around in the flames and not being burned at all! And the three friends weren't tied up any longer! Everyone watching was amazed and knew that God is the Most High God and more powerful than anyone or anything!

Then the king shouted for the friends to come out. (Have kids stop rustling the streamers and direct the friends to emerge.) **King Nebuchadnezzar told the people that God was more powerful than anything and that no one should speak badly of God!**

Yeah! Have kids rustle their streamers in the air and cheer. Ask:

★ **Do you think the three friends set a good example of leadership for the people? Why?**

★ **In what ways did the friends serve God? encourage others?**

★ **Why do you think God saved Shadrach, Meshach, and Abednego?**

★ **What good things came about because of the friends' good example?**

★ **What can we learn from this story about saying no and being loyal to God?**

Write the friends' names on three paper footprints. Then have children list leadership qualities of the three friends on the other footprints. Suggest words such as *loyal, good examples, prayer, bravery,* and *love.* Tape the pairs of footprints to the wall beside those for Moses and Deborah.

Say: **The three friends had to have been scared—who wouldn't be? But they didn't crumble and give in! They were loyal to God and trusted him to make things turn out according to his plan. What good examples of great leadership for God! Let's set more good examples by serving others in the name of God. We can finish up our service project and give others a chance to walk in the footsteps of God's leaders.**

Set aside the crepe-paper streamers; you'll use them in a later activity.

THE MESSAGE IN MOTION

Before class, photocopy the gift card from page 126. You'll need a card for each pair of shoes, socks, or other footwear collected during your drive. Cut pairs of ribbons the size of shoelaces for kids to thread along with the shoelaces on pairs of shoes collected. Satin ribbon works best for this activity.

Have kids work in pairs or trios and lace the shoes collected with ribbons. Leave the regular shoelaces in place and lace the ribbons over them. Tie the laces and ribbons in pretty bows. Some of the kids may prefer to tie ribbons around slippers and socks, while others may wish to color and cut out the gift cards, then tape them to the footwear.

As kids work, have them discuss in their small groups why setting good examples for others shows that we're leaders for God. Encourage kids to name who we can set good examples for, including friends, family, schoolmates, neighbors, and people at church. Then read aloud the gift cards and Romans 10:15. Ask kids what they think the verse means and what good news we can bring to others.

When the footwear is all ready for giving, say: **You've done a wonderful job with this service project, and I'm so proud of you all! Doesn't it feel great to serve others and God at the same time? We'll make sure that people who need these items get them—and the hugs you're sending from God! When we set good examples of being God's servant leaders, others see God's love through us.** Read aloud 1 Timothy 4:12, then ask:

★ **How can we set examples of God's love through our actions? our speech? our lives and love?**

★ **How can you set a better example for your friends and family?**

Say: **We can set a good example as servant leaders for God through our words, actions, and love. Learning God's Word is yet another good example we can set! Let's review our Mighty Memory Verse and discover more about being good examples for God.** Deliver the footwear to a social service agency in your area and let the kids know when the delivery has been made.

SUPER SCRIPTURE

Be sure the Scripture map from last week is still attached to the wall. If you need to make a new map, refer to page 43 for directions. You'll also need one Scripture strip for Romans 8:28 (page 127) for each child.

Gather kids and repeat Romans 8:28 two times, once using the Scripture map and once without it. Then challenge kids to see how many can repeat Romans 8:28 without help. Then hand each child a Scripture strip for Romans 8:28 and tape the strip on a crepe-paper streamer. As kids work, ask:

★ **How did God help things turn out for good for the three friends in the story today?**

★ **Did they love and obey God according to his will? Explain.**

★ **How can setting good examples help things work out for good?**
Say: **Shadrach, Meshach, and Abednego trusted God to work things out the way he chose. The friends said God could save them if he chose to, but even if God chose not to save them, they would stay loyal to God! Yeah!** Have children rustle their streamers like pompons. **That set a powerful example for all the people watching! And in the end, all the people knew of God's saving power because these three friends had been loyal servant leaders. I know that Shadrach, Meshach, and Abednego thanked God for his help, and we can, too. Let's share a prayer and thank God for his grace as we ask his help in always setting good examples of leadership.**

A POWERFUL PROMISE

Have kids sit in a circle holding their paper streamers. Ask for a moment of silence, then say: **We've learned so much today about being servant leaders for God. We've discovered that leaders are loyal to God and set good examples for others. And we worked on the Mighty Memory Verse, which says** (pause and encourage kids to repeat the verse with you), **"And we know that in all things God works for the good of those who love him, who have been called according to his purpose." Romans 8:28.** Repeat the extra challenge verse if you've worked on it with older kids.

Hold up the Bible and say: **Let's make a promise to God to always set good examples of service and leadership in whatever we say and do so that others can know God's power and love. As we pass the Bible around our circle, let's say, "I will set a good example with my words and actions, Lord."** Pass the Bible until everyone has had a chance to make a promise.

Before kids leave, allow five or ten minutes to complete the Whiz Quiz from page 62. If you run out of time, be sure to do this page first thing next week.

Say: **Let's end our time together by serving God with a song! We can rustle our streamers in rhythm as we sing "When I Work" to the tune of "This Old Man."** Refer to page 25 if you've forgotten the words.

End with this responsive good-bye:

Leader: **May you be a strong leader for the Lord!**

Children: **And also you!**

Distribute the Power Page! take-home papers as kids are leaving. Thank children for coming and encourage them to keep their promises to God this week.

POWER PAGE!

8 The Book of Numbers?

Not exactly, but there are lots of numbers in the story of Shadrach, Meschach, and Abednego. Read the questions and the verses in Daniel, then draw lines to the correct numbers.

★ How many feet tall was the idol (3:1)   9

★ How many feet wide? (3:1)   3

★ How many times hotter was the furnace? (3:19)   4

★ How many men were tossed in the fiery furnace? (3:24)   1

★ How many men did the king see? (3:25)   7

★ How many gods do we serve? (You know that answer!)   90

EXAMPLE WHEEL

Color the wheel, then close your eyes and put your finger on the wheel. Set a good example by doing whatever you've chosen. Use the Example Wheel once a day for a week to set ample examples!

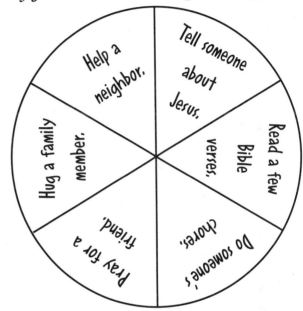

Use Romans 8:28 to fill in the missing high and low letters.

High & LOW

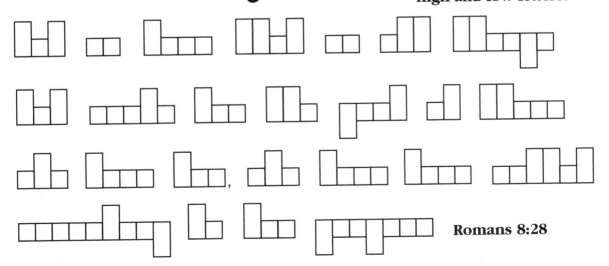

Romans 8:28

WHIZ QUIZ

Color in T (true) or F (false) to answer the questions.

➤ Moses obeyed God. (T) (F)

➤ God only wants some of us to be leaders. (T) (F)

➤ Good leaders also follow. (T) (F)

➤ Deborah praised God for victory. (T) (F)

➤ Setting good examples isn't important. (T) (F)

➤ Leaders are loyal to God. (T) (F)

AIM THE ARROWS

Draw arrows to place the words in their correct positions to complete the Mighty Memory Verse. The first word has been done for you.

God   the   And   that   things   good

all

we   And ____ ____ ____ in ____

____ works for ____ ____ of ____

been

know   who ____ him, ____ have ____

____ ____ to his

those

purpose   ____ . Romans __ ; ___

who

love   called   8   according   28

SERVANT LEADERS IN THE NEW TESTAMENT

I tell you the truth,
whatever you did for one of
the least of these brothers of
mine, you did for me.
Matthew 25:40

PAUL IS CHANGED

We become changed through serving.

John 2:1-11
Acts 9:18

SESSION SUPPLIES

★ Bibles and heart stickers

★ two clear drinking glasses

★ a pitcher of water and food coloring

★ purple construction paper

★ vinyl fabric in a variety of colors

★ black construction-paper foot-prints and a white crayon

★ tacky craft glue and tape

★ scissors and newsprint

★ small safety pins

★ fine-tipped permanent markers

★ 8-inch felt squares and a 6-by-3-foot piece of felt

★ photocopies of the Power Page! (page 71)

MIGHTY MEMORY VERSE

I tell you the truth, whatever you did for one of the least of these brothers of mine, you did for me. Matthew 25:40

SESSION OBJECTIVES

During this session, children will

★ understand that God wants us to serve

★ learn that serving the Lord changes us

★ explore the ways Paul was changed

★ recall that we serve the Lord when we serve others

BIBLE BACKGROUND

We've all heard the saying, "One good turn deserves another." But think for a moment about the *feeling* of that good turn: an encouraging word you've spoken that elicits a smile, or a kind action offered or service rendered that really helps someone in a tough spot. It's that spark of love and genuine satisfaction born of serving someone that begins deep inside, then grows into the fiery desire to help more, serve more—love more. That's what serving the Lord does! It changes us from people of complacency and inaction into salient servants of the Lord who want to give, help, and *do* more! When Paul was changed through Jesus' power on the road to Damascus, he also changed his actions and attitudes from hurting to helping, persecuting to praising, and suffering to serving. And Paul certainly didn't stop at one good turn! He continued to grow, change, and serve the Lord throughout his entire life—and, in turn, he helped multitudes of people change for Jesus!

In today's world of plenty, it's often easy for kids to become self-absorbed in their own needs and wants at the expense of others. It's not that they're trying to disregard others; rather, it's a lack of awareness and experience in putting others first. Use this lesson to help your kids realize that changes in our feelings and attitudes come from serving the Lord and that when we serve others, we're also serving Jesus.

POWER focus

Before class, practice this slick trick so your presentation will be smooth. You will need a sheet of dark purple construction paper, two clear drinking glasses, purple food coloring (or a few drops of red and blue coloring), and a small pitcher of water. Before showing kids the presentation, place a few drops of coloring in the bottom of one of the drinking glasses, then set the glass on the sheet of matching construction paper. (No one will be able to see the drops in the bottom of the glass!) Pour water into the other glass and, at the appropriate time, pour the clear water into the glass containing the food coloring drops. The water will become changed in an amazing way! (Hint: Only have enough water in the pitcher for one full glass of water! Repeating the trick with more water won't work.)

Before kids arrive, place the construction paper on a table with a pitcher of water. Set the glass containing the food coloring drops on the paper along with the empty drinking glass. (Don't let kids see the insides of the glasses!) As kids arrive, welcome them warmly and invite them to tell about times they might have changed their attitudes, thoughts, wishes, plans, or dreams. Encourage them to tell how the changes were brought about and how they felt after they were changed.

Then say: **We read about a lot of changes in the Bible. In fact, Jesus' first miracle was all about serving and changing. Jesus served his friends when they ran out of refreshments by taking plain, old water** (pour water into the empty glass) **and changing it into wine!** (Pour the clear water into the glass with the secret food coloring drops.) **Wow! What a change occurred in the water when Jesus served his friends! Did you know that we change as a result of serving, too?** Ask:

★ **How do we become changed when we love and obey Jesus?**

★ **In what ways do these changes affect the way we treat others?**

Say: **Today we'll be learning that serving others and God changes us in wonderful ways. We'll see how one man was forever changed when he obeyed Jesus and began serving others in Jesus' name. And we'll begin a new Mighty Memory Verse that teaches us even more about serving others.**

First, let's discover how a man who didn't love Jesus became changed forever in surprising—and powerful—ways!

THE MIGHTY MESSAGE

Before class, cut pieces of colored vinyl fabric into ovals that resemble fish scales. Old vinyl tablecloths or place mats will work well. Textured vinyl adds a wonderful tactile touch to this activity. You'll need to cut seven scales for each child.

POWER POINTERS

Help kids make a Before & After list of words that describe how Paul was (and how we are) changed after knowing, loving, and serving Jesus.

Have kids sit in a circle, then say: **Our Bible story today comes from the book of Acts in the New Testament. The story is about a man named Saul, who loved God but didn't love Jesus. Saul didn't believe that Jesus was God's Son or had been raised from death. Saul wouldn't believe that Jesus was alive—and he didn't want other people hearing about Jesus! So Saul traveled around finding Christians and putting them in jail or stoning them for their beliefs. He was a really rotten guy and was blinded to faith, love, and trust in Jesus!**

One day Saul and a couple of his friends were on their way to the city of Damascus. Saul was going there to put more Christians in jail. All of a sudden, there was a blinding light from heaven! Have kids shield their eyes and fall to the ground. **Saul fell to the ground and closed his eyes in fear. Then he heard a voice say, "Saul! Saul! Why do you torment me?" Who do you think spoke to Saul?** Pause for kids to tell their ideas, then continue. **Saul asked, "Who are you, Lord?" And Jesus replied, "I am Jesus, whom you are persecuting. Go to the city and you will be told what to do." So Saul stood up and opened his eyes, but he could not see! Something like**

scales were on Saul's eyes! Hand each child two vinyl scales to hold over his eyes, then ask:

★ **How do you think Saul must have felt?**

★ **Do you think Saul was changing or had been changed? Explain.**

★ **How can we know when someone has changed on the inside?**

Say: **Saul obeyed Jesus and went to Damascus, where he met a man named Ananias. Ananias had been told by Jesus to place his hands on Saul that he might again see and be filled with the Holy Spirit. And at once, something like scales fell from Saul's eyes, and he could see!** Have kids let their scales drop. **Saul spent the rest of his life serving Jesus by telling and teaching others about Jesus' love and forgiveness and about the Holy Spirit. And Paul helped others by setting up churches so more Christians could praise and worship the Lord!** Ask:

★ **By what actions did Paul show he was changed?**

★ **How did Jesus use Paul to serve him? to serve others?**

★ **How are we changed when we serve Jesus?**

Say: **Saul did a lot of changing after accepting Jesus into his life! Even his name changed from Saul to Paul, and Paul is the apostle who wrote many of the New Testament letters or books, such as Ephesians, Galatians, Colossians, and Philippians. Paul spent his entire life serving Jesus and changing for the better! Let's list some of the ways Paul changed on these scales. Then we'll see if serving others can change us, too!**

Hand kids each five more scales and use fine-tipped permanent markers to write on the vinyl scales words that describe how Paul changed. Include words such as *loved Jesus, served others, changed name, had faith, trusted Jesus,* and *knew the Holy Spirit.* As kids work, visit about how we change in the same ways when we serve the Lord.

In addition, write Paul's name on a paper footprint. Then have children list the ways Paul changed to become a good servant leader on the other footprint. Tape the footprints to the wall beside the earlier ones.

When all the writing is complete, help kids poke a small safety pin through the top of each scale to make a zipper-pull or a pin to wear on shoes and clothes. Explain that the pins can be attached to the end of a zipper, hooked on shoelaces, or worn on shirts or jackets as reminders of how we're changed when we serve the Lord and others. Have children attach their scales to their clothing.

Paul

Loved Jesus

Served others

Say: **Paul spent many years serving the Lord through serving the church. We can put the same kind of serving into practice as we begin a new project to serve our church!**

THE MESSAGE IN MOTION

Before class, you'll need to gather materials for this week's portion of the service project. Kids will be making a large banner to present to the church to hang in a sanctuary, an entryway, or a hallway. For this week's portion, you'll need an 8-inch felt square for each child (use various colors), the markers from the previous activity, tacky craft glue, and scissors. You'll also need a very large length of felt or other sturdy fabric for the background of the banner. Colors such as off-white, white, tan, and pastel yellow work well. This length of fabric needs to be five to six feet long and at least three feet wide. Refer to the finished picture on page 84 to get an idea of what you'll be making. To help you get started this week, you'll be adding only the felt hands.

Have kids form pairs or trios and hand each child a square of felt. Explain that for the next three weeks you're going to make a banner for the church and that you'll begin today by making handprints to add to the banner. Encourage the kids to help each other use markers to trace the outlines of one of their hands on the felt, then cut out the felt hands.

Glue the hands in one of two patterns, depending on your class size. For small to medium-sized classes, arrange the hands in a heart pattern. You may need to have kids make two felt hands if your class is very small. For large classes, you may need to make a circle pattern. Be sure to arrange the hands in a pleasing shape and color pattern before gluing them in place. Remember to glue the felt hands with any ink marks facing down so they won't show.

When the felt hands are glued in place, carefully slide the banner aside to dry. Say: **It's fun to serve, isn't it? I'm sure that Paul enjoyed serving God and others as much as we do! Now let's have some fun serving God by learning a new Mighty Memory Verse.**

SUPER SCRIPTURE

Before class, write the words to the Scripture chant below on newsprint. Tape the newsprint to a wall or door for kids to read later.

Help kids find Matthew 25:40 in their Bibles, then read the verse aloud two times. Break the verse into three sections and have kids repeat back each section. Say: **"I tell you the truth"** (pause for kids to echo this portion), **"whatever you did for one of the least of these brothers of mine"** (pause for echo), **"you did for me."** Pause as kids repeat the last portion. Say: **This is a powerful verse, and I'm going to show you what it really means, but first I need three volunteers to help.**

Invite three volunteers to come forward, then shake hands with the first person, hug the next person, and tell the last person, "I love you!" Then ask kids to tell who you shook hands with, hugged, and told "I love you." Say: **You're right! But I also said and did the same things to someone else. Who could that be?** Allow kids to tell their ideas, then continue: **When I do something for or say something to someone, I'm also saying and doing it for Jesus! And that is what Matthew 25:40 is telling us. God wants us to know that whatever we say or do is also being said or done for Jesus.** Ask:

★ **How does knowing this change the way you might treat others?**

Say: **When we're kind and good to others and treat them with respect, we're being kind, good, and respectful to Jesus as well. And if we're selfish and say unkind things to someone, we're also being unkind to Jesus. That makes whatever we say to or do for others very important, doesn't it?**

Repeat the verse three more times in unison, then have kids read the words to the Scripture chant aloud. Invite kids to find partners, then repeat the words to the Scripture chant aloud as you perform the accompanying motions. Repeat the rhyme several times, substituting new actions such as "Give your partner a clap, clap, clap," "a little bow," "a great big smile," and "a friendly hug."

> *Give your partners a cool high five,*
> *And do it just as nice as can be—*
> *Always remember that Jesus said:*
> *"If you did it for them,* (clap-clap)
> *You did it for me!"*

After several repetitions, give each child a quick hug and say, "I'm so glad you're here!" Then say: **It's great to know that when I hug each of you,**

I'm also hugging Jesus! Paul discovered that, when he was kind and helpful to others, he was also treating Jesus the same way. And Paul also discovered how much we change when we're kind to others and serve the Lord. Let's share a prayer asking God's help in treating others kindly and in changing to become better servants. We'll use the scales we made earlier to help.

A POWERFUL PROMISE

Have kids sit in a circle holding two of their vinyl scales. Ask for a moment of silence, then say: **We've learned today that God wants us to serve others and also him. We've discovered that serving the Lord changes us in wonderful ways. And we've worked on the Mighty Memory Verse, which tells us that whatever we say or do for someone else, we say or do for Jesus. Matthew 25:40 says** (pause and encourage kids to repeat the verse with you), **"I tell you the truth, whatever you did for one of the least of these brothers of mine, you did for me."**

Say: **God wants us to serve him and others through our actions, kind words, and loving deeds. And we've learned that serving others changes us in good ways, as it changed Paul. As we pass the Bible around our circle, let's say, "I want to serve you, Lord, with my words and actions."** Pass the Bible until everyone has had a chance to make a promise.

Say: **Place two of your scales over your eyes so you can't see. Then, with your eyes closed, think of what the world would be like without kindness, love, help, and encouragement.** Allow several moments of silence, then quietly say: **When I count three, we'll remove the scales and open our eyes. Then we'll think of how wonderful we feel looking through new eyes that are changed because of serving the Lord. Ready? One, two, three!**

After kids open their eyes, share a prayer thanking God for the chance to serve others and to be changed so we're more like Jesus. Challenge kids to give several of their scales away to others this week as they serve those people with changed hearts full of love and caring.

End with this responsive good-bye:

Leader: **May Jesus' love be with you.**

Children: **And also with you!**

Distribute the Power Page! take-home papers as kids are leaving. Thank children for coming and encourage them to keep their promises to God this week.

POWER PAGE!

ARRANGE a CHANGE!

Jesus arranged a huge change for Paul! From his name to his attitude, Paul changed for Jesus. Change one letter each time to change the first word into a new word.

★ hate   (Paul before Jesus)

★ __ate   (fruit of the palm tree)

★ Da__e   (short for David)

★ d__ve   (white bird)

★ __ove   (Paul after Jesus)

Now unscramble the letters you added to discover how Jesus helped Paul change.

Jesus __ __ __ __ e __ Paul!

What's Changed?

Circle the changes in the second picture.

Now list 3 ways Paul changed for Jesus!

1. _____

2. _____

3. _____

DROPPED VOWELS

The Mighty Memory Verse is missing all the vowels. Use Matthew 25:40 to fill in the missing letters. The first one is done for you.

I t_ll y___ th_ tr_th, wh_t_v_r y___

d_d f_r _n_ _f th_ l__st _f th_s_

br_th_rs _f m_n_, y___ d_d f_r M_.

M_tth_w 25:40

A CHILD SHALL LEAD THEM

MIGHTY MEMORY VERSE

I tell you the truth, whatever you did for one of the least of these brothers of mine, you did for me. Matthew 25:40

(For older kids, add in James 2:22: "You see that his faith and his actions were working together, and his faith was made complete by what he did.")

We can serve with what we have!

John 6:1-13
Matthew 5:3-11; 7:12
Psalm 100:2

SESSION SUPPLIES

★ Bibles
★ bread and tuna salad
★ plastic knives and forks
★ paper plates and napkins
★ a picnic basket
★ black construction-paper footprints
★ a white crayon
★ construction paper
★ scissors and markers
★ tacky craft glue and tape
★ magazines and newsprint
★ self-adhesive letters and string, yarn, or twine
★ photocopies of the Power Page! (page 79)

SESSION OBJECTIVES

During this session, children will
★ realize that even kids can serve
★ discover that serving requires giving
★ learn that we need to be prepared to serve
★ ask God's help in being servant leaders

BIBLE BACKGROUND

"A little child will lead them" (Isaiah 11:6). Perhaps the most powerful example of servant leadership with the right attitude was demonstrated by a young child. In John 6, we read how one young boy shared his food with Jesus and five thousand hungry people. Stop for a moment to consider how most adults serve. Often it's through a sense of guilt, duty, or reluctance and not with the gladness of heart we're called to serve (Psalm 100:2). Yet in John 6 we discover a child who could have easily kept his food for himself, which would have been very childlike, leading the way to serving freely, with gladness, and with purity of heart. What a powerful lesson to learn from the heart of a child!

Kids are often overlooked when it comes to leading the way. After all, they're not adults yet; what could they possibly know about giving freely and serving others? Plenty! Kids need to understand that sometimes the most powerful feats are accomplished through the heart, hands, and hope of a child. Use this lesson to encourage kids to take a leadership role in serving God and others—no matter what they may or may not think they have to offer!

POWER FOCUS

Place a container of tuna salad, a loaf of bread, plastic forks and knives, a paper plate, napkins, and a picnic basket on a table. Explain to kids that you're going on a Bible-story picnic and that they need to be prepared by making picnic sandwiches to share. Have kids work in pairs or trios and assign each a task. Have one set of partners use forks to put tuna salad on slices of bread. (Use one slice for every four kids.) Have another group add the tops to the sandwiches, then pass them to another set of partners, who can cut the sandwiches in quarters. Have another set of partners place the sandwiches on a paper plate in the picnic basket.

When the sandwiches are prepared, ask:

★ **What things can you prepare for when going on a picnic?**

★ **What do we prepare for in life, such as for work, school, or helping others?**

Say: **We prepare for many things each day. We bathe, dress, and even brush our teeth when we prepare to go outside. We prepare for tests in school by studying. And we prepare dinner plans each day. Today we'll discover that we need to be prepared to serve God as well. We'll learn that serving also means giving and that God helps us serve in amazing ways! And we'll also discover that even kids can be servant leaders! In fact, the Bible says, "A little child will lead them"** (Isaiah 11:6). **That's pretty awesome, isn't it?**

Now let's take a hike to get to the picnic grounds where we'll hear an exciting story of how one little boy served the Lord by sharing his lunch with a bunch of people—and with Jesus!

THE MIGHTY MESSAGE

Before class, cut slits in sheets of construction paper (see illustration on page 74). Then cut 2-by-9-inch strips of red, yellow, purple, brown, and blue con-

struction paper. You'll need one of each color strip for
every child. Use a paper cutter to cut the strips
in a snap. Kids will be weaving colorful place
mats during this activity. Place the sheets of
paper and paper strips at one end of the
room or wherever you choose to tell the Bible
story. If the weather is nice, consider going out-
doors for this portion of the lesson! Be sure you have a pair of footprints to add to your display from the past several weeks. (See page
40 if you need to make new footprints.)

Have kids follow you in a lively march to the place you've chosen to
tell the Bible story and weave the place mats. When you arrive, say: **That
was quite a march! Did you know that about five thousand people
walked, hiked, marched, and came to hear Jesus teach one fine day?
They came to sit on a hillside and listen to Jesus teach
about God and how God wants us to live. Jesus taught
them many things, such as the Beatitudes and the
Golden Rule.** Read aloud Matthew 5:3-11; 7:12. **And Jesus
taught them about serving one another through his
own examples of kindness and teaching.**

**Everyone learned so much that day, but when
the sun was setting, the people were very hungry!
They hadn't eaten all day, and there was no food
in sight! Even Jesus' disciples were worried about
what they would do.**

Choose a child to stand and hold the picnic basket,
then continue: **Then Andrew saw a boy holding a basket! There were two loaves of bread and five fish in
his basket. Could that feed five thousand hungry tum-
mies?** (Pause.) **When Jesus is serving, it can! The little
boy served Jesus by offering his food to share. Then
Jesus gave thanks for the food and fed every hungry
tummy there.** Hand out the sandwiches and let kids nibble them as you finish
the Bible story. **When they were done eating, Jesus told the disciples to collect the leftovers, and there were twelve baskets full of bread and fish!
What a feast—and all because a child served by sharing his food!**

As kids finish their treats, have them discuss the qualities the boy in the
story had, such as giving, generosity, willingness, prepared to serve, and love.

POWER POINTERS

Challenge kids to take over one typically adult chore to show that kids can serve as powerfully as grown-ups! Kids might carry out the trash, rake the yard, or even fold the wash.

little boy

prepared to serve love

Write some of the words on one of the footprints and write "little boy" on the other. Tape the footprints to the wall by the footprints from previous stories.

Hand each child a sheet of paper with slits and a paper strip of each color. At the end of each question, kids will weave a paper strip into their place mats.

★ **What examples of serving did Jesus demonstrate?** (After the answers, tell kids to weave a purple strip into their place mats to represent Jesus and how he taught us about serving.)

★ **How did the little boy serve God and others?** (Tell kids to weave a yellow strip into their place mats to represent the value of giving to others and God.)

★ **How much did the boy have to share? How did God help make it more?** (Instruct kids to weave a blue strip into their place mats for the water fish swim in and for the boy's giving of fish to feed the people. Then add a brown strip to represent the bread he gave.)

★ **What can we learn about serving from this story?** (Tell kids to weave a red strip into their place mats to represent the love we show whenever we give and serve!)

Tape the ends of the paper strips to the place mats. As kids are finishing, say: **The little boy didn't have much to share, did he? Especially when there were so many people in need. But he came prepared, and God worked in a miraculous way and used what the little boy gave to serve many! Wow! Now that is God's multiplication! Just think, it doesn't matter how old we are or how much we have to give. God will use us when we're prepared, then multiply the blessings!**

The little boy gave food to serve God and others. We can give through our time and talents to serve God and others as we add the next pieces to our cool banners! Set the place mats aside until the Super Scripture.

THE MESSAGE IN MOTION

Before class, you'll need to purchase self-adhesive letters to add to the banner. Purchase vinyl or fabric letters and be sure to purchase several sets so you'll have enough letters to write the following verse: "Serve one another in love. Galatians 5:13." You'll also need a 3-foot length of string, yarn, or twine and tacky craft glue.

Have kids form several small groups and assign each group several words to Galatians 5:13b (including the reference), then have kids collect those letters from the packages of self-adhesive letters. Do not remove the paper backings just yet. Designate two kids to be the rulers and have them sit on either side of the banner and hold the length of string in an arc over the hands. Use the string as a baseline for placing the words to the Scripture verse. Have kids arrange the letters before they remove the paper backing and secure the letters in place. If any letters are misplaced, carefully remove them, then glue them to the banner in the correct position. Write the verse at the top of the banner; place the Scripture reference at the bottom.

Serve one another in love.

Galatians 5:13

When kids finish writing the verse, set the banner aside and ask:

★ **How can our one banner serve many people?**

★ **In what ways are we giving to others as we serve them by making this banner? How are we giving to God?**

★ **What difference do you think this banner might make in helping others?**

Say: **Just as a bit of bread and fish didn't seem like a lot to give, one banner may not seem like a lot either. But God multiplies our service when we honor him by serving others. Our banner will be an encouragement to many people, a good reminder about serving others, and even a way to say "We love you" to God and our church! No matter how old we are, no matter how much or how little we have, we can always find ways to serve God and others!**

Let's serve God in a different way right now. We'll serve God by learning his Word as we make cool place mats to help us remember the words to our Mighty Memory Verse!

SUPER SCRIPTURE

Before class, you'll need to collect magazines that contain pictures of food items. Each child will need several pictures, so be sure you have a good selection of magazines!

Gather kids and introduce the Mighty Memory Verse by repeating the action rhyme you learned last week. Review the words with kids, then have them find partners and repeat the rhyme, adding new action verses such as "Give your partner a clap, clap, clap," "a little bow," "a great big smile," and "a friendly hug." If there's time, let kids invent new actions to go along with the words.

Give your partners a cool high five,
And do it just as nice as can be—
Always remember that Jesus said:
"If you did it for them, (clap-clap)
You did it for me!"

After several repetitions, have kids repeat Matthew 25:40 three times. If you have older kids who have already mastered Matthew 25:40, introduce the extra challenge verse (James 2:22). Then ask:

★ **How are we to treat others? In what ways are we treating Jesus the same?**

★ **How does knowing this verse help us serve others? give to others?**

Say: **This verse teaches us that whatever we do for someone else, we do for Jesus, too! In other words, if we serve someone else, we serve Jesus. If we're kind and giving to others, we're kind and giving to Jesus. That's pretty simple—and that's pretty important, too! When the little boy in the Bible story gave his food to serve others, he was also serving Jesus. Let's use food to help us remember this important Mighty Memory Verse.**

Have kids cut out food items and write "Serve others" across the tops of the place mats and "Serve Jesus!" across the bottoms of the place mats. When the place mats are finished, you may wish to cover them in clear self-adhesive paper to protect them.

Say: **Use your pleasing place mats during meals to remember how the little boy shared what he had as he served God and others—just as we can give and serve no matter what we have. Let's serve God right now with a prayer thanking him for multiplying what we do in his name and for helping us serve him.**

A POWERFUL PROMISE

Before class, write the words to the song in this activity on newsprint and tape it to a wall or door for kids to read as you sing.

Have kids sit in a circle and ask for a moment of silence, then say: **We learned so much about being servant leaders today. We learned that we can serve God no matter how old we are and no matter what we have to give. We also discovered that giving is a part of serving. And we worked on the Mighty Memory Verse that teaches us that whatever we do for someone else, we do for Jesus. Matthew 25:40 says** (pause for kids to repeat the verse), **"I tell you the truth, whatever you did for one of the least of these brothers of mine, you did for me."** If you worked on the extra challenge verse, have kids repeat it.

Hold up the Bible and say: **God has promised he will help us in all things. And we know that God helps us serve just as he helped the little boy serve Jesus and others by sharing his food. It didn't seem like much, but it made all the difference! As we pass the Bible around our circle, we can make our own special promises by saying, "I want to serve with all I have, God."** Pass the Bible until everyone has had a chance to make a promise. End with a prayer thanking God for multiplying the service you give to others, then thank him for his divine help as you seek to serve. End with a corporate "amen."

Say: **Psalm 100:2 tells us to "serve the Lord with gladness; come before his presence with singing"** (KJV). **The little boy in today's story served God as he gladly gave his food to be shared. We can gladly share a song as we serve God. Let's sing this serving song to the tune of "Row, Row, Row Your Boat."** Invite kids to make up actions for the line "short or tall or spring or fall." Once kids are familiar with the words, sing the song in a round.

Serve, serve, serve the Lord
With gladness in your heart.
Short or tall or spring or fall—
Now's the time to start!

End with this responsive good-bye:
Leader: **May you serve with all you have!**
Children: **And also you!**

Distribute the Power Page! take-home papers as kids are leaving and remind them to take home their place mats. Thank children for coming and encourage them to keep their promises to God this week.

POWER PAGE!

THROUGH GOD'S HELP

Jesus served 5,000 through a miracle from God. What other miraculous ways did Jesus serve others? Draw matching lines between the Scripture references and the ways Jesus served.

John 2:1-11 — *calmed the sea and his disciples' fears*

Luke 5:1-11 — *changed water to wine and helped his friends*

Mark 4:35-41 — *cured sickness and healed a leper*

Matthew 8:1-4 — *helped fishermen catch a lot of fish*

Feeding 5,000?

Well, not quite that many! But this super supper will serve your family and friends in a big way!

TUNA-N-TOAST CASSEROLE

Mix two cans of drained tuna, 2 cups of shredded cheese, 1 can of cream of mushroom soup, and ¼ cup of chopped onion. Toast 12 pieces of bread, but don't butter them! Layer the toast and tuna mixture in a pan and sprinkle with extra cheese. Bake at 350 degrees for 30 minutes.

High & LOW

Fill in the high, low, and in-between letters to complete Matthew 25:40.

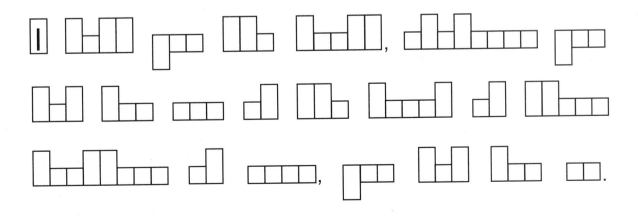

PRISCILLA AND AQUILA SERVE

We can serve the church with our gifts and talents.

Acts 18:1-28
James 2:22

SESSION SUPPLIES

★ Bibles
★ white paper and markers
★ black construction-paper footprints
★ a white crayon
★ scissors and tape
★ gold satin cord
★ gold tassel trim
★ dowel rods
★ tacky craft glue
★ photocopies of the Whiz Quiz (page 88) and the Power Page! (page 87)

MIGHTY MEMORY VERSE

I tell you the truth, whatever you did for one of the least of these brothers of mine, you did for me. Matthew 25:40 *(For older kids, add in James 2:22: "You see that his faith and his actions were working together, and his faith was made complete by what he did.")*

SESSION OBJECTIVES

During this session, children will
★ learn that we can serve many people at once
★ realize the importance of serving at church
★ understand we're part of God's family
★ praise God for the opportunity to serve him

BIBLE BACKGROUND

Church services are held at 8:00, 10:00, and 11:00. What goes through most people's minds when they think of church services? Is it how the church will serve them or their family's needs through sermons, fellowship, and programs the church has to offer during the week? Wouldn't it be refreshing and wonderful if the first thought that came to mind from the phrase *church services* was: *How can I offer my services to the church? What needs of the church can I help fulfill?* Priscilla, Aquila, Apollos, and Paul, as well as countless missionaries and volunteers, have taught us richly about the responsibilities we have in being part of God's church family. With Jesus as the head of the church and Matthew 25:40 reminding us that what we do for others we do for Christ, how can we do less than serve the church with glad hearts and compassion?

Kids are just becoming a part of what they recognize as their "church family." And just as in their families at home, kids need to be aware of ways to serve their church family members with love, generosity, and hard work! Use this lesson to help kids understand that even the smallest acts of serving touch many lives when they serve the Lord at church!

POWER focus

Welcome kids and have them stand in a circle. Explain that you're going to start off with a rousing game of Multiple Simon Says in which they'll be following one or more actions at the same time. Give the following Simon says commands, interspersed with a few commands in which you don't say "Simon says."

Simon says:

★ *touch your nose and close your eyes*

★ *hop on one foot and wave to a friend*

★ *twirl two times in place and clap three times*

★ *whistle a tune and skip once around the circle while clapping*

★ *hold your elbow, hop up and down, and nod your head*

★ *give someone a high five, then smile and say "I'm glad you're here!"*

★ *sit in place, put your hands in your lap, and hum quietly*

When everyone is seated, say: **That was fun and you all did a great job of doing many things at one time!** Ask:

★ **Is it easy or hard to do many things at once? Explain.**

★ **Can we do a good job when we're doing many things at one time? Why or why not?**

★ **Why is it great that God can love many people at one time?**

★ **Are we able to love many people at once? help many people at once?**

Say: **It's impossible to do more than one thing at a time in some cases, such as when we're studying. It would be pretty difficult to study math, spelling, and reading all at the same time! But there are times when we can do many things at once, like when we help at home by cooking dinner. By that one action, we can feed several family members. Or when we clean litter off the streets, we are helping many people enjoy the outdoors even more and serving God by keeping his world beautiful. It's the same way at church. When we pitch in and serve at church, we're touching many people's lives at one time.**

Today we'll explore how we can serve at church and touch many people at once. We'll discover that we're all part of God's family at church and that family members serve one another. We'll also be exploring our Mighty Memory Verse, which teaches us that whatever we do for someone else, we do for Jesus! Now let's hear a wonderful story of two people who served in one of the first churches and helped many people all at the same time.

THE **MIGHTY** MESSAGE

Before class, practice cutting out lines of paper dolls. Follow the illustrated directions to get the basic routine, then tape three sheets of paper together to make one long piece of paper. Fold the long paper into nine equal portions, then cut out a paper doll. When you open up the folds, you should discover nine dolls linked together! Be sure you have a set of black footprints for this week's Bible story leaders. See page 40 if you need to make new ones.

Just before class, tape and fold your long paper. Lightly draw the paper doll cutting lines on the paper to help guide you, then cut out the dolls at the appropriate time in the story.

Place the scissors and paper beside you. Hold the folded paper and say: **Our Bible story today comes from the book of Acts. It takes place after Jesus had been raised from death and told his disciples to go into all the world to baptize others in his name and to teach them about loving God and about eternal life. As I tell the story, I'll be cutting this paper. But you can help by remembering the** names of people from the story. Hold up a finger each time I mention a person's name in the story.

Begin slowly cutting out the paper doll as you say: **Long ago, the church was just getting its start. Not many people knew about Jesus and his forgiveness, so churches were springing up to spread**

POWER POINTERS

Ask a church leader or worker if your class can pitch in to serve the church, such as with a yard-cleaning, bathroom-redecorating, or library-cleaning job.

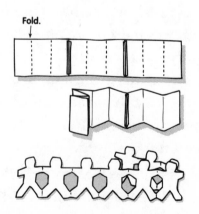

Fold.

the Good News and to provide places for believers to gather. **One wife and husband, Priscilla and Aquila, lived in a city called Corinth.** Pause, then ask: **Who were the wife and husband?** Have kids tell their names, then continue the story and the cutting.

Priscilla and Aquila loved Jesus and wanted to serve him. One day Paul came to town. Paul had been traveling everywhere to set up churches and teach others about Jesus. Pause, then ask: **Who came to town?** After kids tell Paul's name, continue. **Paul needed a place to stay, so Priscilla and Aquila gladly offered their home to Paul. Paul stayed with Priscilla and Aquila and taught them even more about Jesus. Then they all sailed to Syria, where Priscilla and Aquila met a man named Apollos who wanted to know more about Jesus.** Pause, then ask: **Who did Priscilla and Aquila meet?** After kids tell Apollos's name, say: **So Priscilla and Aquila taught Apollos about Jesus and they introduced Apollos to Paul. And soon these four went on to teach more and more people the Good News about Jesus and to establish more and more churches!**

Finish cutting the paper doll if you haven't already. Hold up the doll and say: **Just as I cut out one paper doll and brought many together** (open up the line of paper dolls), **so one act of serving brought many people together! Priscilla and Aquila's act of serving by giving Paul a place to stay and by teaching about Jesus touched many lives!** Ask:

★ **How did Priscilla and Aquila serve Paul? Apollos?**

★ **In what ways did they serve Jesus? people in churches?**

★ **How can doing something to serve in our church help many people?**

Say: **Isn't it wonderful that one act of serving can multiply to help many people? When we give our time, our talents, and our money to help the church, we're helping all the people who go to our church. We're also helping get ready for all the new people who will come to our church—and we're serving God at the same time. Wow! That's a lot of serving, isn't it?** Ask:

★ **What are ways to serve at our church?**

★ **How can serving at church encourage others to do the same?**

★ **In what ways does helping others at church draw us closer to them? closer to God?**

Have kids think of servant-leader qualities portrayed by Priscilla and Aquila, then list them on one of the footprints. Write Priscilla's and Aquila's names on the other and tape the footprints to the wall with those you have been collecting over the past several weeks.

Then say: **I'm glad that Priscilla and Aquila were a family who loved God! Did you know that we're all part of God's family and part of our church family? And we know that it's great to serve our families! Just look!** Hold up the paper dolls. **See how they're joined together? That's just what happens when we serve our church family. We become joined together with one another and with God! There are lots of ways to serve in church, and one way is by finishing the cool banner we've been working on!** Set the paper dolls aside until later.

THE MESSAGE IN MOTION

Before class, collect two 3-foot-long dowel rods that are 1-inch in diameter. You'll also need 3 or 4 feet of gold tassel trim and a 3-foot length of gold satin cord to use as a hanger. If you plan to present your gift to the church today, make prior arrangements with the minister to find a time to bring the banner into the sanctuary or wherever you plan to hang it. Be sure to explain that it won't be ready to hang for a day or so until the glue dries.

Place the banner face down on the floor. Run a line of tacky craft glue along the length of the banner, about 2 inches from the bottom. Do the same across the top of the banner. Stick the top and bottom edges of the banner in the glue to make rod pockets. Have kids all help hold the edges securely on the glue while it sets. Challenge kids to count to one hundred, then repeat the Mighty Memory Verse two times.

Carefully slide the dowel rods into the rod pockets, then gently turn the banner over. Run a line of tacky craft glue ½ inch from the bottom and stick the gold tassel trim to the glue. Finally, tie the ends of the gold cord to the ends of the top dowel rod. Glue the knots in place on the dowel rod.

As you let the banner dry for a few minutes, discuss how it feels to have a lovely gift to present for the whole church to enjoy. Then explain to kids that the banner will be hung when it is dry but that today you'll present the banner to the church, then lead everyone in a prayer. Ask for a volunteer to lead a prayer for the congregation. If no one is comfortable leading a prayer, have everyone repeat the Mighty Memory Verse as a good reminder about serving others and Jesus, too.

After you've presented your gift, say: **It's so wonderful to serve our church in special ways—and this banner will remind everyone about serving. Just like Priscilla and Aquila, we were able to touch many lives with one act of serving! That's pretty awesome, isn't it? Let's serve God right now by showing him how much we love learning his Word as we review the Mighty Memory Verse.**

SUPER SCRIPTURE

Have kids find partners and invite pairs to repeat the Mighty Memory Verse. If partners have trouble or forget a portion of the verse, let them call on someone to serve them by reminding them. If you have older kids, repeat the process with the extra challenge verse. Continue until everyone has had a chance to repeat the verse.

Hand each child two sheets of paper and show kids how to tape the paper end to end to make one long sheet. Then demonstrate how to fold the paper for paper dolls. Let kids trace a paper-doll pattern on their papers, then cut out the dolls. Help younger kids draw and cut their dolls or encourage other kids to serve those having trouble.

When the dolls are cut out, have kids write the Mighty Memory Verse on one doll, then write one way to serve at church on each of the remaining paper dolls. Ways to serve might include cleaning the yard, emptying wastebaskets, stuffing envelopes, or cleaning the church kitchen, if there is one. When the dolls are complete, have kids form small groups and share the ways they've thought of to serve at church.

Say: **Priscilla and Aquila helped with the early church. And because they loved Jesus so much, they wanted to serve him, too. They served Jesus in a powerful way by helping Paul, Apollos, and other early Christians. Priscilla and Aquila did for Jesus what they did for the people they served, just as our Mighty Memory Verse teaches us.** Ask:

★ **What can you do this week to serve at church?**

★ **How is serving at church also a way to serve the Lord?**

Say: **When we serve our church family, we're also serving Jesus! Again, we can touch many through one act of serving, just like Priscilla and Aquila. And when we serve, our faith and love for the Lord are put into action! Listen to what the Bible says about faith and action.** Read aloud James 2:22 and ask older kids if they recognize the verse (it's their extra challenge verse!). Then say: **When we love the Lord and have faith in his** help, we're able to serve others in wonderful ways—and our faith is put into action! Let's offer a prayer of thanks and praise to God for helping us continue to discover ways to serve at church, at home, in our community, and in the world.

A **POWERFUL** PROMISE

Have kids sit in a circle and ask for a moment of silence. Quietly say: **We've learned so much about serving in the church today. We discovered that we can serve many with even one act of kindness. We learned that we are all part of God's family and our church family, and we explored different ways to help at church. And we reviewed the Mighty Memory Verse, which says, "I tell you the truth, whatever you did for one of the least of these brothers of mine, you did for me. Matthew 25:40." There are many wonderful verses in the Bible that teach us about serving. I'd like to read three of them while we bow our heads in prayer. As I read, think about how good God is to help us find new ways to serve each day.**

Read aloud the following verses, then end with "amen."

Serve one another in love. (Galatians 5:13)
Serve wholeheartedly, as if you were serving the Lord, not men. (Ephesians 6:7)
Whatever you do, whether in word or deed, do it all in the name of the Lord Jesus, giving thanks to God the Father through him. (Colossians 3:17)

Say: **God wants us to serve others, and he promises to help us find ways to serve when our hearts are willing. As we pass the Bible around our circle, let's make a promise of our own to God. When it's your turn, say, "I am ready and willing to serve you, God."** Pass the Bible around the circle until everyone has had a chance to make a promise.

Before kids leave, allow five or ten minutes to complete the Whiz Quiz from page 88. If you run out of time, be sure to do this page first thing next week. End with this responsive good-bye:

Leader: **May you serve the Lord with gladness.**

Children: **And also you!**

Distribute the Power Page! take-home papers as kids are leaving. Thank children for coming and encourage them to keep their promises to God this week.

POWER PAGE!

**Use the words in the word bank
below to complete Matthew 25:40.**

CHURCH SERVICE

**Priscilla and Aquila served the early
church and Christians. Discover who
else served the church by reading the
references and filling in the names.**

Acts 13:2, 3   _ _ _ _ _ _ _ ◯

Romans 16:1, 2   _ _ _ _ ◯ _ _

Acts 13:4, 5   _ _ ◯ _ _ _

Philippians 2:25-30

_ _ _ _ _ _ _ _ ◯ _

Acts 18:24-28   _ _ _ _ _ _ ◯

*Now unscramble the circled letters to dis-
cover who else these people served.*

_ _ _ _ _ _

_ tell _ _ the _ _ _ _ _, whatever

you did _ _ _ one of the _ _ _ _ _ of

these _ _ _ _ _ _ _ _ of mine, you

_ _ _ for _ _ .

Word   Bank

me   you   whatever

least   brothers   I

for   truth   did

Fill 'Er Up With Thanks

1 2 3 4 5

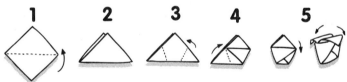

Send a cup full of thanks to
someone who serves in your
church. Fold a paper cup
according to the illustrations,
then cut out the poem and
glue it to the cup. Finish by
decorating the cup with
markers and crayons. Read
Matthew 6:1-4 to find out
how to present your special
thank-you.

LOTS OF LOVING THANKS!

Here's a paper cup to fill you up
With thanks and lots of love—
You serve so true in all you do
For our church and God above!

WHIZ QUIZ

Color in T (true) or F (false) to answer the questions.

➤ Paul didn't really need to change.   (T) (F)

➤ We can serve in many ways.   (T) (F)

➤ Paul was changed by Jesus' love.   (T) (F)

➤ Priscilla and Aquila served Jesus.   (T) (F)

➤ Churches don't need our help.   (T) (F)

➤ Serving God is always easy.   (T) (F)

➤ Not all of us can serve others.   (T) (F)

Follow the arrows to plug in the missing letters from Matthew 25:40.

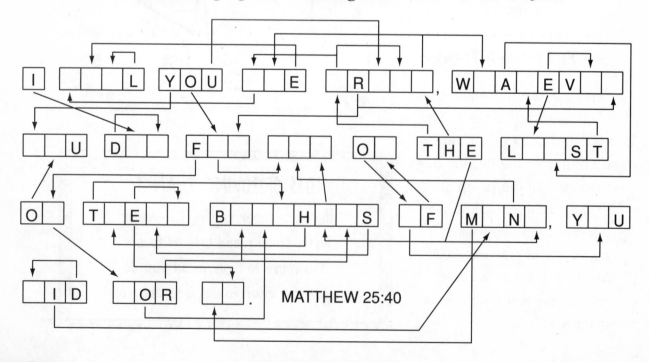

MATTHEW 25:40

SERVING TODAY!

Therefore go and make
disciples of all nations,
baptizing them in the name of
the Father and of the Son
and of the Holy Spirit.
Matthew 28:19

MISSIONARIES IN MOTION

Missionaries serve God in many places.

Acts 10:36-44

13:1–14:28

SESSION SUPPLIES

★ Bibles

★ a bouncy playground ball

★ a world map or map of Paul's travels

★ newsprint and markers

★ tape and a stapler

★ four sheets of poster board

★ world, globe, or heart stickers

★ photocopies of the Missionary Scavenger Hunt lists (page 124)

★ photocopies of the Power Page! (page 97)

MIGHTY MEMORY VERSE

Therefore go and make disciples of all nations, baptizing them in the name of the Father and of the Son and of the Holy Spirit. Matthew 28:19

SESSION OBJECTIVES

During this session, children will

★ understand that missionaries go into all the world

★ learn that missionaries tell others about Jesus

★ realize we need to support missionaries

★ discover ways to encourage missionaries

BIBLE BACKGROUND

Many Christians have wondered what it would be like to step onto foreign soil as a missionary for Christ, but most have remained stateside for one reason or another. God calls us to serve in different ways, and being a foreign missionary may not be the task God has for you. But remember: God calls all of us to support and encourage one another, and there is a place in foreign missions for each of us without leaving home! By supporting, encouraging, and helping missionaries, we can live a kind of vicarious missions life right alongside servant leaders in foreign lands. We may not be actually witnessing to tribes in Tanzania or healing the sick in Malaysia, but through our gifts of medicine, money, supplies, letters, and prayers we become one in the body of believers and can serve as powerful "missionaries in absentia."

Kids love learning about foreign lands, customs, and people and are open to hearing and learning about the exciting, wonderful work of foreign missionaries. Offer kids the opportunity to join foreign missions as helpers and supporters as they learn that God honors our support as much as our service!

POWER FOCUS

Warmly greet kids as they arrive, then invite them to stand in a large circle. Explain that in this fun and lively warm-up game, you'll toss or bounce the ball to someone in the circle as you name a city, state, or country in the world, such as Madrid, Iowa, or Jamaica. See how long you can continue naming places as the ball travels from one child to another.

When you're all "named out," have kids sit in a circle, then say: **That was fun! Our bouncing ball really traveled around, didn't it? You know, missionaries travel around a lot, too—only they don't just bounce from one place to another, they stay where they are for a while to teach others about Jesus and his message of forgiveness, salvation, and love.** Ask:

★ **Where would you travel to tell others about Jesus?**

★ **What could you tell someone there about Jesus?**

Say: **Today we'll be exploring how real-life missionaries serve God all over the world. We'll discover that some missionaries travel many miles to bring the Good News about Jesus to others, and we'll learn important ways to encourage missionaries while they're away from home. And we'll also learn a new Mighty Memory Verse that Jesus himself told to us.**

Right now, let's learn about the different places Paul traveled in the Bible, then we'll see how one missionary family serves God in an exciting foreign country today! Set the ball aside until later.

THE MIGHTY MESSAGE

Before class, collect a world map or make a large color copy of a map of Paul's missionary journeys from a Bible resource book. Attach the map to the bulletin board or wall so kids can see it. You'll also need a highlighter pen that will show up on the map. Kids will be marking Paul's travels with the pen.

Gather kids in front of the wall map and say: **A few weeks ago we learned about a man who was changed when he began to serve God. His name was Paul. What do you remember about Paul?**

Encourage kids to tell what they remember, then say: **Paul was such an important servant leader because he started many churches in one part of the world, and those churches grew and multiplied. And because of Paul and his diligent serving, we have churches all over the world today in which to learn about and worship Jesus. Paul was one of our first missionaries. That means Paul was someone who took the Good News about Jesus to others. Let's take a look at all the places Paul traveled as a missionary. We'll mark Paul's journeys on our map.**

Have volunteers draw lines as directed in parentheses. **Paul started his first long journey in the area around Antioch, north of Jerusalem, and he sailed to the island of Cyprus to tell others about Jesus.** (Draw a line from Antioch to Cyprus.) **From here, Paul and his missionary friend Barnabas sailed to Perga in Pamphylia** (pamFILLeeya) **to teach about Jesus.** (Draw a line from Cyprus to Pamphylia.) **After one of Paul's friends went back to Jerusalem, they moved northward to the region of Pisidia, where there was another city called Antioch.** (Draw a line from Pamphylia to Antioch in Pisidia.)

Paul went to a synagogue, or Jewish place of worship, there and told the Jews about Jesus and his message of forgiveness. The people there became angry at Paul and didn't want to hear the wonderful news because they didn't believe Jesus was God's Son. So Paul turned his attention to the Gentiles—people who didn't know God or Jesus. Many of these Gentiles believed and were baptized! Paul was so excited!

Next, Paul and Barnabas went to the cities of Iconium and Lystra, where Paul healed a crippled man. (Draw a line from Antioch in Pisidia to Iconium, then to Lystra.)

Then the missionaries went on to Derbe, before retracing their footsteps and returning home. (Draw a line from Lystra to Derbe, then retrace the trip back to Antioch north of Jerusalem.)

POWER POINTERS

Correspond through email or regular mail with a church-sponsored missionary or one chosen from Internet listings. Both your kids and the missionary will love making and encouraging new friends!

Whew! Paul and Barnabas traveled very far to tell others about Jesus and to set up churches and encourage churches already going. And that's not all! Paul spent the rest of his life going here, there, and everywhere to teach about Jesus! He even went to Rome, where he was finally killed for believing in Jesus. Even when times were hard and people wouldn't listen, Paul kept serving the Lord in powerful ways as a missionary. Ask:

★ **How was being a missionary a way Paul demonstrated his love for God?**

★ **Why do you think Paul never quit, even when it was hard being a missionary?**

★ **What could you have said to Paul to encourage him?**

Say: **Missionaries are very important servant leaders! They tell others about Jesus, they teach about God, they help people build churches and schools, and they pray with and for others. Listen to what missionaries tell others about Jesus.**

Read aloud Acts 10:36-44, then say: **It's not always easy being a missionary, and they need lots of support! We can support missionaries today and encourage them in their important work. So let's begin a brand new service project to help missionaries in another country serve God and others.**

THE MESSAGE IN MOTION

Before class, choose a missionary in a country outside your own. See if your church hosts a missionary and use this person or family. Or search the Internet under the category "missionaries" to identify listings for postal and email addresses of missionaries. You'll also need to photocopy the Missionary Scavenger Hunt lists on page 124. Make plenty of copies—you'll be sending some home with the kids and stapling the rest to posters the kids will make today.

Have kids form four groups and explain that each group will be hunting for and collecting different items to send to a missionary. Tell kids the missionary's name and where she is serving. Assign one team to be the school-items group, one to be the Bibles-n-books group, another to be the clothing group, and the last team to be the personal-care group. Hand the hunt lists

Give a Little— Serve a lot!

Bring in your donations today!

School Supplies

Take a list and collect the items to help our missionary. Thank you!

to their corresponding groups and have kids read their list of items aloud. Explain that items can be collected for the next two weeks and brought to class. Tell kids that they can bring in as many different items from the lists as they'd like and that duplicate items are wonderful!

Then have each group make a poster advertising their part of the Missionary Scavenger Hunt. Let kids decorate their posters to reflect items that need to be collected, then staple the hunt lists to the posters for others to take as they collect their donations. Add snappy poster titles such as, "Give a Little—Serve a Lot!" or "Serving Takes a Moment—Giving Lasts a Lifetime!"

When the posters are complete, hang them where adults in the congregation are sure to see them, such as in the church entryway or in a hall. Then gather kids and ask:

★ **Why is it important to help missionaries?**

★ **What are other ways we can support and encourage missionaries?**

Say: **Gathering items missionaries can use to serve others is one way to support them. And praying for missionaries is another way to support and encourage these wonderful servant leaders. Let's pray for the missionary we've chosen to help.**

Lead kids in a prayer thanking God for your "adopted" missionary. Pray that your service project will be a great success and that people will open their hearts with donations to help you help your missionary introduce people to Jesus and his saving love. End with a corporate "amen."

Say: **Not everyone can travel to foreign countries to be a missionary. But everyone can help support the missionaries who do travel to serve God. I'm glad we can be a part of helping a missionary, too! Now let's learn a new Mighty Memory Verse that Jesus gave us to remind us of the importance of going into all the world as servant leaders.**

SUPER SCRIPTURE

Before class, draw the Scripture map on a large sheet of newsprint or poster board and attach it beside the map you used in The Mighty Message.

Gather kids in front of the Scripture map and point to each

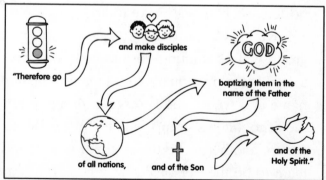

portion of the verse as you repeat it. Discuss how the pictures represent what is being said in each verse portion, then have kids take turns coming to the map and pointing as they repeat the verse.

When everyone has had a chance to use the Scripture map, say: **Jesus said these words just before he returned to God in heaven. In this verse, Jesus commanded us to be servant leaders who take the message of his forgiveness all around the world and who baptize people as believers in Christ. That's a pretty important command. We call it the Great Commission, and we want to be committed in bringing the Good News of Jesus to people all around the world! That's where missionaries come in.**

Right now I'd like to tell you about the Harris family, who are missionaries in Nakurur, Zaire, a country in eastern Africa. The Harrises have only been in Zaire a short time. John and Martha have two kids: Annie, who is ten, and William, twelve. The family teaches the Africans many things about Jesus but say they've learned just as much themselves, especially about perseverance, patience, and God's protection! In fact, not long ago the Harrises had a firsthand experience of God's protective grace. One day they tried to open the door to the hut they live in, but it would not budge. They tried several times during the day, but the door would not open, so they used a window in the back instead. The next morning, the door opened with ease, and they saw why God had kept it shut the day before: right under the first step was a freshly shed skin from a poisonous snake! The Harrises know that the Lord helps them every day and ask your help in praying for the encouragement of all missionaries worldwide.

Say: **It takes patience, perseverance, courage, and lots of love to become a missionary to other parts of the world. But God helps missionaries, and we can, too! Let's share a prayer asking God to help missionaries in their work and making a promise to look for ways to encourage missionaries wherever they serve.** Save the Scripture map to use next week.

A POWERFUL PROMISE

Before class, write the words to the missionary song in this activity on newsprint and tape the words to the wall or a door for kids to see. Be sure you have world, globe, or heart-shaped stickers.

Have kids sit in a circle and ask for a moment of silence, then say: **We've learned today that missionaries go all over the world to teach others** about Jesus and his message of forgiveness and salvation. We've discovered that God helps missionaries and that we can help and encourage them, too. And we began to learn a new Mighty Memory Verse that Jesus gave us, in which he commands us to go into all the world and teach others to obey God. Matthew 28:19 says (pause and encourage children to repeat the verse with you), **"Therefore go and make disciples of all nations, baptizing them in the name of the Father and of the Son and of the Holy Spirit."**

Hold up the stickers and say: **God promises to help missionaries in their work. And we can be willing to help them, too. Let's promise to support and encourage those people who take the Good News of Jesus into all the world! We'll pass these stickers around the circle. After making your promise, put a sticker on your hand to remind you that we're all missionaries when we tell others about Jesus' love! For our promise, let's say, "I want to help your missionaries, God."** Continue around the circle until everyone has made a promise and has a sticker. Then end by sharing a prayer asking God's help with missionaries and their work. Ask for God's wisdom in work and safety in travel, then thank God for providing brave missionaries such as Paul to take the Good News into all the world.

Say: **Let's end by singing a missionary song about serving. We'll sing the song to the tune of "B-I-N-G-O," and on the second time around, we'll clap in place of the letters to the word** *serve.*

If you think you've got the nerve,
Then go for God and start to serve!
S-E-R-V-E!
S-E-R-V-E!
S-E-R-V-E!
Then go for God and start to serve!

End with this responsive good-bye:
Leader: **May you always be willing to go for God!**
Children: **And also you!**

Distribute the Power Page! take-home papers as kids are leaving and remind them to take home their scavenger hunt lists and to return the items next week. Thank children for coming and encourage them to keep their promises to God.

POWER PAGE!

TRAVEL-TRIP

Draw a map of your neighborhood, town, or state to show where you can go to tell others about Jesus.

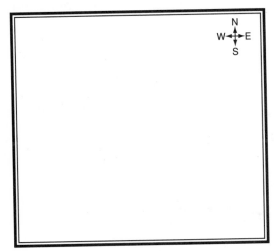

Draw a ♥ on the first place you'll go!

Scrambled Lands

Unscramble the names of these lands, then fill in the letters at the bottom to discover where Jesus told us to serve others.

ewN Zlendaa __ __ __ __ __ __ __ __ __ __
                  1   3

carAfi __ __ __ __ __ __
      2   9

naFrce __ __ __ __ __ __
      4   8   12

Gmanyre __ __ __ __ __ __ __
      5

htoSu leoP __ __ __ __ __ __ __ __ __
        6 10 11   7

__ __ __ __ __ __ __ __ __
5 6 9 8 10 6 2 7 7

__ __ __ __ __ __ __ __ .
10 11 12 1 6 4 7 3

 **Fill-'em-In**

T __ __ __ __ __ F __ __ __ __ , __ __

and make __ __ S __ __ __ __ __ __ __

of all __ __ T __ __ __ __ __ ,

__ __ __ T __ __ __ __ __ them in the

__ __ __ __ __ of the F __ __ __ __ __

and of the __ O __ and of the

__ O __ __ Spirit.

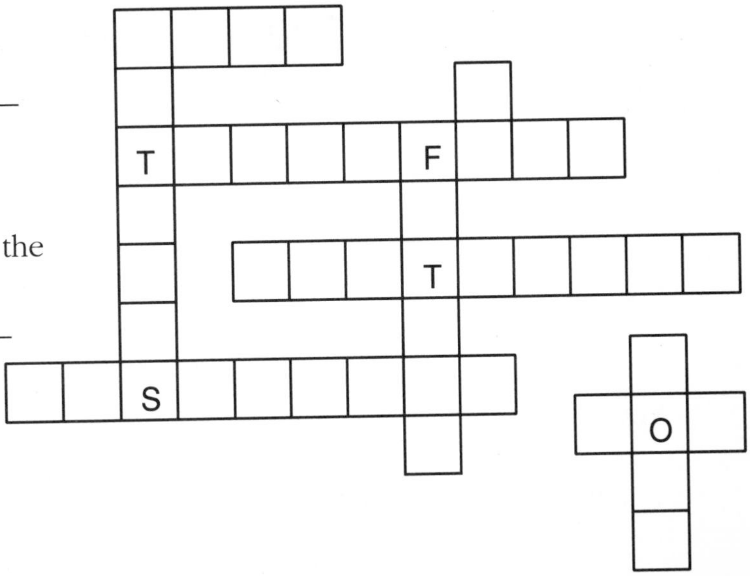

Use Matthew 28:19 to fill in the missing words to the Mighty Memory Verse. Then fill the words in the puzzle grid.

(crossword grid with letters T, F, T, S, O)

We can be
missionaries to
our families.

Ruth 1:1–2:23
Acts 10:42
Romans 10:17

SESSION SUPPLIES

★ Bibles
★ self-sealing sandwich bags
★ cereal, raisins, and chocolate
chips
★ a mixing bowl and spoons
★ scissors, index cards, and
markers
★ clear tape and ribbon
★ wheat or grasses from a
craft store
★ four sturdy boxes
★ gift wrap and newspaper
★ photocopies of Matthew
28:19 (page 127)
★ photocopies of the Power
Page! (page 105)

SERVING AT HOME

MIGHTY MEMORY VERSE

Therefore go and make disciples of all nations, baptizing them in the name of the Father and of the Son and of the Holy Spirit. Matthew 28:19

(For older kids, add in Matthew 28:20: "And teaching them to obey everything I have commanded you. And surely I am with you always, to the very end of the age.")

SESSION OBJECTIVES

During this session, children will
★ learn they can be missionaries to families and friends
★ discover why serving family members is important
★ explore ways to serve their families and friends
★ offer thanks for missionaries around the world

BIBLE BACKGROUND

Have you ever heard of the saying, "The cobbler's family goes barefoot"? We often display the same negligence when it comes to serving our own families and closest friends. It's easy to give money at church to support missionaries and missions projects. It doesn't take much planning to offer a quick prayer for missionaries in foreign lands or to donate a blanket to a missions drive. But when it comes to our families and friends, serving is often not seen as separate acts of selfless giving. It's often neglected or pushed aside as serving ceases to be an act of giving and turns into dull duty. It's important to recognize the needs of our families and to strive to serve each member in the spirit of gladness and love that God commands. Just think if the cobbler took the time to make his family shoes—wouldn't they be the most beautiful shoes on anyone's feet? And just think if we served our families in the same way—wouldn't they be the most beautiful smiles of all on people's faces?

Kids need to understand that serving their families and close friends is as important as serving others in foreign lands but is often overlooked and under-practiced! Use this lesson to raise kids' awareness that our families are our first missionary stops and that when we serve our families and friends, we're serving our loving Father as well!

POWER focus

Before class, purchase a variety of crunchy cereals such as frosted corn flakes, oat rings, fruit rings, and crispy rice cereals. You'll also need raisins, chocolate chips, and any other munchy ingredients you'd like, such as sunflower and pumpkin seeds or miniature marshmallows. Pour all the ingredients into a large mixing bowl and toss the ingredients with a spoon. Set the bowl on a table with plastic spoons and self-sealing sandwich bags. Set a stack of index cards and markers at one end of the table.

Before kids arrive, cut index cards in half and draw pairs of simple pictures on the cards. Use pictures such as suns, stars, hearts, flowers, kites, and swirls. If you prefer, use matching pairs of stickers on the cards.

Greet kids and hand each a card with a picture. Tell kids not to show their cards to anyone but to look at the picture and remember what it is. Then have kids gather around the table with the goodies. Explain that in this activity, they'll be making a bag of munchy-crunchy Missionary Mix to share with the person who has a matching picture card. Tell kids that after they prepare a bag half full of mix, they can design a card to go with the goodies. Have children either write encouraging words on the card, write something that tells about Jesus, or draw a colorful picture. As kids work, ask:

★ **Does it make a difference in how we serve when we don't know the person we're serving? Explain.**

★ **How is this like serving people we don't know in our cities or in other countries?**

★ **In what ways can we serve and encourage people we don't know? people we do know?**

When the treat bags and cards are finished, have kids find a place to put their items until later, when the secret servers are revealed.

Say: **God wants us to be willing servants in all we do. Last week we learned about missionaries in foreign lands and how they serve people they don't even know. Today we'll learn about being missionaries here at home to our own families and friends. We'll discover that serving our families and friends is not unlike serving in foreign countries and that when we serve in love, we're also honoring God in love! And later, we'll discover who your secret server is when we share our yummy Missionary Mix treats! Right now, let's explore how one family in the Old Testament served in love, willingness, and generosity—just the ways God wants us to serve!**

POWER POINTERS

Consider having children invite their family members into class to share extra Missionary Mix treats, then teach them the serving song.

THE **MIGHTY** MESSAGE

Before class, collect stalks of dried wheat or dried decorative grasses from a craft store, florist shop, or field. You'll need at least ten stalks for each child. Cut 8-inch lengths of ribbon, one for each child.

Before this activity, scatter the dried wheat or grasses around the area, then have kids sit in the center of the room. Invite kids to tell about ways they help, serve, support, and encourage family members and friends. Ways might include sharing chores, being a good listener, reminding them of Jesus' love, and praying for them.

Say: **In our story today, a young woman named Ruth married into a family and became very dear friends with her husband's mom, Naomi. When the men in the family died, Naomi encouraged Ruth to return to her real mom in her real family. But Ruth wanted to stay with Naomi. You see, Naomi had told Ruth about God and his love, and Naomi had shown Ruth much love as well. So Ruth decided to stay with Naomi, and they served one another by sharing chores and their love of the Lord as well.**

Naomi and young Ruth decided to return to Naomi's home in Bethlehem. But when the two women arrived, they were very hungry. They had no money, so Ruth went to glean wheat in the fields. When the harvesters were done, Ruth would go along and pick up the snippets of wheat and wheat stalks left behind in the field. See if you can each glean ten stalks of wheat in our classroom.

When everyone has ten stalks, continue. **Ruth served Naomi by gathering the wheat so they could bake good bread to share. In return, Naomi helped Ruth find a good husband! Ruth, her husband Boaz, and Naomi made a fine family who served one another and worshiped God with love.** Ask:

★ **In what ways did Ruth serve Naomi?**

★ **How did Ruth demonstrate her love through serving?**

★ **What good things happen when families and friends serve one another?**

★ **How does serving draw families closer to God? to each other?**

Say: **When we think of serving others, we often think of people in hospitals, foreign countries, or friends at church. That's good, but sometimes we forget that we're to serve our families as well.** Ask:

★ **Why is serving our families important?**

★ **What are ways to serve our family members?**

Say: **We have the families we live with, and we're also part of a family here at church. Why, our own class is even like a family! Earlier you made Missionary Mix treats and cards for a secret someone. Now we'll make pretty wall hangings from the wheat stalks to give to our secret friends, too!**

Have kids tape the wheat or grass bundles together in the center, then tie ribbons around the tape. When the sheaves are complete, have kids place them with their treat bags and cards. Say: **It's fun to serve, isn't it? And just wait until later when we discover who our secret servers are! But now, let's practice more serving with our Missionary Scavenger Hunt project.**

THE MESSAGE IN MOTION

Before class, select four sturdy boxes to decorate. You'll be using these boxes for mailing, so be sure they're sturdy. Packing boxes available at moving centers are wonderful! You'll also need festive gift wrap, tape, newspapers, and scissors.

Have children get into their serving teams and wrap the items they brought. Wrap small items such as pencils and erasers or rulers together. If you run low on wrapping paper, Sunday newspaper comics make cute gift paper! As kids work, ask questions such as, "How are we related to missionaries through God's family?" and "How do you think it helps missionaries to know that someone wants to encourage them?"

When the items are wrapped, gently layer them in the boxes with wads of newspaper. Save room to add more items to the packages next week if more items are donated.

Say: **Last week we heard about a real-life missionary who is serving in Zaire. Today let's learn about another missionary family, this one in Florida.**

The Palmeras family lives in south-central Florida, where they serve as missionaries to the Seminole Indians who live in the area. They love the Seminoles and say they are the friendliest people they have ever met, with hearts eager to know Jesus and follow him. The Palmeras family includes George, Maria, and their kids Lina, Juanita, and little Daniel. They all spend many hours with the Seminoles and enjoy the sweet-sounding arrow flutes the Seminoles play at times during worship. The Palmeras family also enjoys helping each other by listening to one another, helping around the small house they live in, and teaching each other fun crafts such as weaving sweetgrass baskets, which the Seminoles taught them how to make. Their favorite part of the week is drawing Secret Pal names in their family and doing nice things in secret for their family pals. The Palmeras family says that serving their family is as important as serving others—and makes God smile!

Even missionaries serve in their families and support and encourage one another. And since we're all part of God's family, we can serve each other and God, too! That's pretty awesome! I know another great way to serve God. Let's review our Mighty Memory Verse and add one more part to our secret server gifts!

SUPER SCRIPTURE

Before this activity, make sure you have the Scripture map from last week. Tape the map to the wall or a door so kids can see it easily. You'll also need photocopies of the Scripture strip for Matthew 28:19 (and verse 20, if you desire) from page 127.

Gather kids in front of the Scripture map and repeat Matthew 28:19 twice. (If you have older kids, introduce verse 20 as well.) Then challenge kids to come forward, stand beside the Scripture map, and try to repeat the verse without looking at the map. If they need help, they can take a sneak-peek at the map, then continue. Encourage each child to participate, then give everyone a lively round of applause.

Say: **It's important to understand what this verse is saying to us. Remember, Jesus said these words to his disciples just before ascending to heaven. What was Jesus telling his disciples and us to do in this verse?** Invite kids to share their thoughts, then ask:

★ **Why is it so important for others to know Jesus?**

★ **How do missionaries play an important role in bringing others to Christ?**

Read aloud Romans 10:17, then say: **Jesus wants to be sure everyone in the world has a chance to hear the Good News about his forgiveness and salvation. But the world is so big, it will take each of us to help accomplish that goal! Some people are missionaries in foreign lands, but we can also be missionaries to our families and friends right here.**

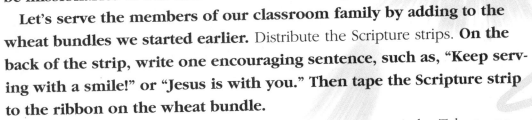

Let's serve the members of our classroom family by adding to the wheat bundles we started earlier. Distribute the Scripture strips. **On the back of the strip, write one encouraging sentence, such as, "Keep serving with a smile!" or "Jesus is with you." Then tape the Scripture strip to the ribbon on the wheat bundle.**

When the bundles are finished, have everyone sit in a circle. Take turns having kids exchange their bundles, Missionary Mix bags, and cards with the secret server whose picture card matches theirs. Encourage kids to respond with rousing thank-yous for being supported and served. Then say: **Now I challenge each of you to continue serving by passing along one of the items you received to someone in your family or to a friend this week! And now, let's offer the Lord a prayer of thanksgiving for servant leaders all over the world.**

A **POWERFUL** PROMISE

Ask for a moment of silence, then say: **We've learned today that servant leaders support and encourage their families and friends. We've discov-**

ered that it's important to take Jesus' message of love and salvation throughout the whole world so others will know, love, and follow Jesus. And we've reviewed the Mighty Memory Verse that says (pause and encourage kids to repeat the verse with you), **"Therefore go and make disciples of all nations, baptizing them in the name of the Father and of the Son and of the Holy Spirit"** (Matthew 28:19).

Hold up the Bible and say: **We've been commanded to tell others about Jesus and his love.** Read aloud Acts 10:42, then continue: **Now we can make our own special promise to do as Jesus commanded by saying, "I will tell others about you, Jesus."** Pass the Bible until everyone has had a chance to make a promise.

Say: **Let's end by singing the missionary song we learned last week about serving. We'll sing the song to the tune of "B-I-N-G-O," and on the second time around, we'll clap in place of the letters to the word** *serve.*

If you think you've got the nerve,
Then go for God and start to serve!
S-E-R-V-E!
S-E-R-V-E!
S-E-R-V-E!
Then go for God and start to serve!

End with this responsive good-bye:

Leader: **May you always be willing to go for God!**

Children: **And also you!**

Distribute the Power Page! take-home papers as kids are leaving and remind them to collect more items from their scavenger hunt lists and to bring the items next week. Thank children for coming and encourage them to keep their promises to God.

POWER PAGE!

Ruth's Date Bread

Ruth made tasty bread to serve her family. Now you can, too!

You'll need:

- ★ 3 cups flour
- ★ 1 cup sugar
- ★ 2 Tbl. oil
- ★ 1 beaten egg
- ★ 1 tsp. salt
- ★ 1½ cups milk
- ★ 4 tsp. baking powder
- ★ 1 cup chopped dates

Directions:

1. Sift dry ingredients together.
2. Mix egg, milk, and oil in a bowl, then add to the dry ingredients. Mix well!
3. Stir in the chopped dates.
4. Bake at 350 degrees for 1 hour, then cool.
5. Slice and *serve* your delicious treat!

GIVE SERVING A SPIN!

Decorate a paper plate as in the illustration. Add your own family chores, then use a pencil and paper clip as a spinner. Let each family member take a spin on the service wheel and pitch in to help!

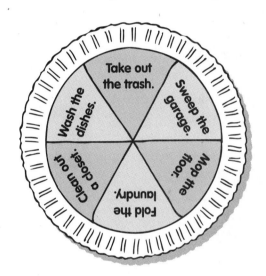

Take out the trash.
Sweep the garage.
Mop the floor.
Fold the laundry.
Clean out a closet.
Wash the dishes.

LETTER BEFORE

Write the letter that comes <u>before</u> the letter under each space to complete Matthew 28:19!

_ _ _ _ _ _ _ _ _ , GO AND _ _ _ _ _ _ _ _ _ _ _ _ _ _
U I F S F G P S F   N B L F   E J T D J Q M F T

OF ALL _ _ _ _ _ _ _ , _ _ _ _ _ Z _ _ _ THEM IN THE
      O B U J P O T   C B Q U J   J O H

_ _ _ _ OF THE _ _ _ _ _ _ AND OF THE _ _ _ AND OF THE.
O B N F   G B U I F S   T P O

_ _ _ _ _ _ _ _ _ _ . MATTHEW 28:19
I P M Z   T Q J S J U

START TO SERVE!

Together we can make a difference in the world!

Exodus 3:4
1 Samuel 3:10
Isaiah 6:8
1 Peter 3:15

SESSION SUPPLIES

★ Bibles
★ construction paper
★ white paper
★ scissors, tape, and gift wrap
★ clear packing tape and shipping labels
★ pencils and markers
★ green sticker dots
★ photocopies of the Good News Newspaper (page 125)
★ photocopies of the Whiz Quiz (page 114) and Power Page! (page 113)

MIGHTY MEMORY VERSE

Therefore go and make disciples of all nations, baptizing them in the name of the Father and of the Son and of the Holy Spirit. Matthew 28:19

(For older kids, add in Matthew 28:20: "And teaching them to obey everything I have commanded you. And surely I am with you always, to the very end of the age.")

SESSION OBJECTIVES

During this session, children will
★ realize that they can change the world for Jesus
★ understand God will help them serve
★ learn that they can be Jesus' ambassadors
★ thank God for his loving help in serving others

BIBLE BACKGROUND

How many requests do you field in a day or a week? Bosses ask us to take on more responsibilities, spouses request us to attend work-related functions, kids demand help on homework or extra money for college, and friends plead for a listening ear *now*. We have so many calls, commands, requests, and questions every day that demand our time and energy! Yet it's not the number of requests that's important, but *how* we choose to respond. God calls for our time and attention, too. In Isaiah 6:8, God asked "Whom shall I send? And who will go for us?" Without the least hesitation, Isaiah responded, "Here am I! Send me!"

Isaiah had a willing heart to serve God and put God before other demands on his time. Isaiah was ready to go for God when God requested action! How we respond when God calls says much about the willingness of our hearts and spirits. And though our time is precious, being able to go for God is most precious of all!

Kids understand the concept of "ready, set, go!" They understand that if you don't get up and go you never reach the goal! Encourage kids to put this natural go-getter attitude to work serving God and help them understand that God calls us into service in many ways.

POWER FOCUS

Before class, cut a large green circle and a large red circle from construction paper. One will be the "go" light and the other the "stop" light.

Warmly greet kids and have them gather at one end of the room. Explain that you'll begin your time with a lively game to get the wiggles out and to

see how good everyone is at stopping and going. Stand at the end of the room opposite the kids and show them the red and green "traffic lights." Explain that when they see the green light, they can move forward walking heel-to-toe, but when the red light is showing, they must stop and freeze in place. Continue stopping and going until the first few kids reach you. Then have a child hold the circles and go to the opposite end of the room to play again. Repeat the game several times, designating new ways to move and new stop-light holders.

When the game is finished, applaud kids' efforts, gather everyone in the center of the room, and ask:

★ **What made you get up and go in this game? Explain.**

★ **Did you want to keep moving even on the red light? Why or why not?**

★ **Could you have gotten to your goal if you hadn't sprung into action on the word "go"? Explain.**

★ **How is this game like getting a message from God to go serve or help someone?**

★ **Why is it important for us to get up and go for God? to obey God's commands?**

Say: **We've spent several weeks learning about being servant leaders and discovering what missionaries do and how we can be missionaries right now in our own families. Today we'll see how different kids have served others in real life and how they learned that it's important to go for God. We'll also review our Mighty Memory Verse and finish our missionary service project.**

But right now, let's discover how some real kids found ways to go for God and serve.

THE MIGHTY MESSAGE

Before class, photocopy the Good News Newspaper articles on page 125, one for each child.

Gather kids and say: **Throughout the Bible we read about times God called someone to serve him and how that person responded. I'll read a few examples, and you listen for what the person said or did when God called. When you think you know how that person responded, stand up!**

Our first example is about a young boy whom God called. The boy's name was Samuel, and he wasn't much older than you kids! Listen while I read, and when you know how Samuel responded to God's call, stand up. Read aloud 1 Samuel 3:10, then let kids tell that Samuel responded to God's call by saying, "Speak, for your servant is listening."

Good for you! Let's see how you do with this next one. Our next example is about the time God first called Moses. When you know how Moses responded to God, stand up! Read aloud Exodus 3:4, then let kids tell that Moses responded to God's call by saying, "Here I am."

Wow! You're good detectives! But I have another example. This example is told by Isaiah, and he's telling us about a time God called. When you know how Isaiah responded to God's call, stand up. Read aloud Isaiah 6:8. Have kids tell that Isaiah responded by telling God he was ready to go for him and take his word to others.

POWER POINTERS

If you have time, invite kids to form small groups and to make "Go For God!" posters to hang around the church as reminders to serve God willingly and gladly.

Say: **When God called each of these people, they responded with willing hearts. They showed they were ready to get up and go for God, and that's just the kind of servant leaders we want to be— ready, willing, and able to serve God whenever he calls!**

Now let's form three groups and read about some kids who used their thinking caps to find ways to serve and spread God's love to others! If your class is very large, form six groups and have two groups read each article.

Hand each child a copy of the Good News Newspaper and assign each group one of the articles to read. Instruct group members to answer the questions that appear below their articles. After several minutes, invite groups to share their articles and answers with the whole class.

Say: **These kids and many more like them are changing the world for Jesus, one person at a time! And we can help change the world for Jesus, too, by being strong servant leaders in all we say and do. We can serve right now by finishing our missionary service project and getting our boxes ready to send.**

THE MESSAGE IN MOTION

Set out white paper, markers, and the four large boxes from last week. Have kids get into their serving teams and wrap any items kids have brought in this week. Next, invite kids to either write encouraging notes to your missionary or draw colorful pictures of themselves, the area in which you live, the church, or anything they'd like to send.

As kids work, review the qualities a servant leader needs, such as honesty, faith, love, courage, and a willingness to serve. Refer to the construction-paper footprints if they're still hanging. Remind kids that missionaries are ambassadors for Jesus and they should set good examples of Jesus' acceptance, compassion, and love.

When the items are all wrapped and packed and the letters and pictures are placed in the boxes, seal the boxes with clear packing tape and address them to the missionary you have chosen. Assure kids the packages will be mailed out and should arrive at their destination soon.

Gather kids around the boxes and say: **You've done such a wonderful job with this service project, and I know our missionary will feel loved, encouraged, and very special. Doesn't it feel good to know we can help missionaries and serve God at the same time? In fact, when we become** faithful servant leaders, we can change the world for Jesus and help lots of people know, love, and follow Christ. Our missionary boxes are a good beginning! Let's offer a prayer for the safe delivery of these special boxes, for the missionary who will receive them, and for the people who will be helped by the items.

Have kids join hands around the boxes and pray: **Dear Lord, we're so happy and thankful to be a part of serving missionaries and people in other lands as they get to know you and Jesus. Please watch over these boxes and make sure they reach their destination safely and quickly. We ask that your loving guidance be with missionaries all over the world, and please open the hearts of the people who will be touched by missionaries telling the Good News about Jesus. Amen.**

Let's sing the missionary song we've learned to the tune of "B-I-N-G-O." On the second time around, we will clap in place of each of the letters to the word *serve.*

If you think you've got the nerve,
Then go for God and start to serve!
S-E-R-V-E!
S-E-R-V-E!
S-E-R-V-E!
Then go for God and start to serve!

Say: **Servant leaders are always ready and willing to go for God. And servant leaders know the importance of learning God's Word. Let's review the Mighty Memory Verse as we learn more about being ready to go for God.**

Be sure to mail the boxes out and let children know the approximate date of arrival. For the next several weeks, pray for the missionary, the boxes, and the people who will use the items.

SUPER SCRIPTURE

Before class, purchase green circular stickers from an office supply store. These stickers are often used to code files and folders. Be sure the Scripture map from last week is on the wall. If you need to make a new map, refer to page 94.

Gather kids by the Scripture map and use the map to repeat Matthew 28:19 two times. If you have older kids, also repeat verse 20 two times.

Then have kids line up at one end of the room as you stand at the opposite end holding the green stickers. Ask, "Who will go for God?" Then encourage a volunteer to repeat the Mighty Memory Verse. If the verse is correctly repeated, say, "Go for God!" and have the child run to you and collect a green "go" sticker. If the verse isn't repeated correctly, let the child ask a "servant leader" in class to help with the verse, then continue. When everyone has a "go" sticker, ask:

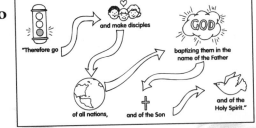

★ **Why is it important for servant leaders to know and use God's Word?**

★ **In what ways does knowing God's Word help us serve others better? help us tell others about Jesus?**

Say: **That was a fun game, and it helped us learn God's Word even better. But speaking God's Word isn't enough. We need to use God's Word, too! Matthew 28:19 tells us to go into all the world to make disciples of others. In other words, we're to go everywhere to serve God and tell others about Jesus.** Ask:

★ **Who can you tell about Jesus this week?**

★ **What can you tell people about Jesus?**

★ **How can our serving actions speak just as loudly as words to others?**

Read aloud 1 Peter 3:15, then say: **We want to serve others in deed and by telling them about Jesus. Let's ask God's help in what we do and say to be good servant leaders.**

A POWERFUL PROMISE

Have kids sit in a circle and ask for a moment of silence, then say: **We've learned today that we can make a difference in people's lives and help them know Jesus through serving. We know that God will help us find new ways to be servant leaders but that we must be ready and willing to go for God when he calls. And we've worked on the Mighty Memory Verse that commands us to go into all the world for the Lord. Matthew 28:19 says** (pause and encourage kids to repeat the verse with you), **"Therefore go and make disciples of all nations, baptizing them in the name of the Father and of the Son and of the Holy Spirit."** (Continue on to verse 20 if you have older kids.)

Hold up the Bible and say: **We know that God will help us serve and bring the Good News about Jesus to others. In return, we can promise to be ready and willing servants for God. As we pass the Bible around our circle, let's say, "I will go for you, God, and be your servant leader."** Continue around the circle until everyone has had a chance to make a promise. End with a prayer asking for God's help in discovering new ways to serve and in being willing to serve when God calls.

Before kids leave, allow five or ten minutes to complete the Whiz Quiz from page 114. If you run out of time, be sure to do this page first thing next week.

Close by singing the missionary serving song and have kids clap and march in time to the rhythm. Sing to the tune of "B-I-N-G-O."

If you think you've got the nerve,
Then go for God and start to serve!
S-E-R-V-E!
S-E-R-V-E!
S-E-R-V-E!
Then go for God and start to serve!

End with this responsive good-bye:
Leader: **May you serve God in all you do!**
Children: **And also you!**

Distribute the Power Page! take-home papers as kids are leaving. Thank children for coming and encourage them to keep their promises to God this week.

POWER PAGE!

GET SERIOUS!

Get serious about serving others! Write a way to serve in each area, then achieve your super service goals one by one.

I'll serve God by _____

_____

I'll serve my family by _____

_____

I'll serve my friend, _____ , by

_____

I'll serve my church by _____

_____

Serving Hands

Make these cool gloves, then use them for dusting, washing the car, weeding the garden, carrying dishes to the table, or any other ways your helping hands can serve.

You'll need:
- 1 pair of cotton gardening gloves
- permanent markers
- craft glue
- plastic watch and jewels

Decorate the gloves with colorful designs, then glue plastic items to your helping hands! *When you serve and share, these are cool to wear!*

CRACK THE CODE!

Use the key below to complete the **MIGHTY MEMORY VERSE**, Matthew 28:19.

_____ , go and _____ disciples of ___

_____ , _____ them in the ____

of the _____ and of the ___ and of the ____

_____ .

A	B	E	F	G	H	I	K	L	M	N	O	P	R	S	T	Y	Z
✿	✓	✱	✖	✦	☆	✪	✎	☐	◆	●	✛	■	✝	♥	↔	✺	➥

WHIZ QUIZ

Draw lines to the correct words for each sentence.

1. Missionaries serve all over the _____ .   **all**

2. Jesus said, "Go into ____ the world."   **serve**

3. It's important to _____ our families.   **God**

4. Ruth served _____ with love.   **missionaries**

5. When we serve others, we serve _____ .   **world**

6. We can support and encourage _____ .   **Naomi**

AIM THE ARROWS

Draw arrows to place the words in their correct positions to complete the Mighty Memory Verse. The first word has been done for you.

disciples   baptizing   go   all

Therefore

Therefore ____ and _____ _____

of ___ _____ , _____ _____

in the _____ of the _____ and of the

___ and of the _____ _____ ,

Matthew __ ; __

them   make   nations   28

Spirit   Son   19   Father

name

Holy

REVIEW
LESSON

And whatever you do,
whether in word or deed, do
it all in the name of the Lord
Jesus, giving thanks to the
Father through him.
Colossians 3:17

SERVANT LEADERS

We become good leaders when we're good followers—of Jesus!

Galatians 5:13
Ephesians 6:7
Colossians 3:17

SESSION SUPPLIES

★ Bibles

★ high-bounce balls (see Power Focus for details)

★ colored permanent markers

★ small powdered sugar donuts

★ vanilla ice cream

★ paper bowls and plastic spoons

★ chocolate and strawberry toppings

★ maraschino cherries

★ photocopies of the continents (page 122)

★ photocopies of the Mighty Memory Verses (page 127)

MIGHTY MEMORY VERSE

This is a review lesson of all four Mighty Memory verses: Colossians 3:23; Romans 8:28; Matthew 25:40; and Matthew 28:19.

SESSION OBJECTIVES

During this session, children will
★ review who we serve and why we serve
★ understand following the Lord is the start of leadership
★ review the qualities of servant leaders
★ praise God for his divine leadership in our lives

BIBLE BACKGROUND

When you take your family to a fine restaurant, how do you expect to be treated? You probably expect service that is kind, warm, and friendly; service that is prompt, amiable and attentive. After all, it's your loved ones being served, and you are paying for the meal. Can God expect any less of us as his servants? God has paid an enormous price for our salvation. And after all, we are called upon to serve his loved ones, who just happen to be our brothers and sisters, too! God wants his servants to be kind, warm, and friendly and to serve in a manner that is prompt and complete, amiable and attentive. In other words, God wants no less of us than what we demand of the diner on the corner—and the "tip" is so much greater! When we serve God and his loved ones with all our hearts, the gracious gratuity lasts forever!

Use this celebratory review lesson to joyously remind kids that they are already God's special servant leaders and have an honorable responsibility to serve God and others the world around in whatever way they can.

POWER focus

Before class, purchase an inexpensive high-bouncing playground ball for each child. Children will be adding neat designs to their bouncing balls during this review lesson and will take the balls home at the end of the lesson. The cost may be a bit more than you usually spend on crafts, but this is a special review lesson, and you want it to be memorable! You'll also need an extra ball to use for this activity.

Greet kids and have them stand in a large circle. Explain that this is a lively game of Follow the Leader. Hold up a ball and say: **In this game, we follow the person holding the ball and do whatever the leader does. When I call out, "switch!" the leader is to quickly toss or bounce the ball to someone else, who will become the new leader. We have to keep moving in this game, and we'll continue until everyone has had a chance to be the leader.**

Start the game by bouncing the ball to a child. Switch leaders every minute or so until everyone has been the leader. Then set the ball aside and ask:

★ **Which was more fun: to be the leader or a follower? Why?**

★ **Which is more important: to be a good leader or follower? Explain.**

★ **In what ways does being good followers of Jesus help us?**

Say: **What would a game of Follow the Leader be without both leaders and followers? You have to have both to make it work. And the same is true for serving the Lord! To be good servant leaders, we need to be good followers of Jesus. That means we need to obey Jesus' commands and follow the examples he gave us of how to treat and serve others.**

Today we'll review all that we've learned in the past few weeks about being servant leaders. We'll discover how to be good followers of Jesus and why that helps us be better leaders. We'll also review the Mighty Memory Verses we've learned to keep them fresh in our minds and lives.

As we review all we've learned, you'll be making way-cool globe balls to remind you that we're to go into all the world to serve others. First, you need some land and water! Toss each child a bouncy ball. Say: **Hold on to your growing globes and don't bounce them until it's time! Now let's review the Bible messages we've learned as we discover more about leading for and following the Lord.**

THE MIGHTY MESSAGE

Before class, photocopy and enlarge the patterns on page 122 on stiff paper, then cut them out. If you have young kids, consider tracing simple outlines of the continents on each ball before class. You may also want to invite several teen or adult volunteers to help during class. If your kids are older, they can trace and color the patterns directly on their globe balls or you can simply enlarge the patterns and hang them on a wall so kids can trace the outlines freehand by looking at the patterns. Otherwise, let kids help each other trace and color the patterns on the balls.

Have kids stand at one end of the room and hold the colorful balls.

Say: **Let's make this a review game. I'll ask a question, and if you think you know the answer, bounce your ball to the end of the room, then sit down gently on it. I'll call someone to answer the question. If that person is correct, she can lead the rest of you back across the room as you follow just as in Follow the Leader! Ready? Listen carefully to the questions!**

★ **What happened to Daniel when he refused to serve anyone but God?** (He was tossed in a lions' den, then saved by an angel of the Lord.)

★ **When we serve others, who else do we serve?** (God; Jesus.)

★ **What did Jesus teach his disciples and us by washing his disciples' feet?** (He taught us about serving others as he served us.)

★ **What did Moses do when God called him to serve?** (Moses obeyed; Moses said, "Here I am.")

★ **What are some qualities of good servant leaders?** (Honesty, willingness, loyalty, love, kindness, courage, and the like.)

★ **How did Shadrach, Meshach, and Abednego set a good example of being God's servant leaders?** (They refused to honor any other god; they were loyal to God; they obeyed God's commands.)

★ **Why is it important to be a willing servant?** (So we can obey God; so we're always ready to help and tell others about Jesus.)

★ **Where did Jesus tell us to go and serve?** (We're to go into all the world; everywhere.)

POWER POINTERS

Photocopy all the Mighty Memory Verses from page 127 on bright neon paper for each child to practice at home in the coming weeks. Remember: reinforcement means memory!

★ **In what ways do missionaries serve others?** (They feed the hungry, tell others about Jesus, teach school, and lead church.)

★ **How can we support and encourage missionaries?** (By donating needed items; by praying for them; by writing letters.)

★ **How can we serve others?** (By helping them; by praying for them; by telling others about Jesus.)

Say: **Wow! You all remembered about serving so well! I'm proud of you, and I know that God must be smiling, too! And since you've shown you understand why and where we're to serve, you can add your first pieces of the world to your globe balls.**

Have kids use permanent markers to add and to label North and South America on their globe balls. When the continents have been colored in, say: **You're on your way to going all around the world. Our next stop will be for a super serving celebration!**

THE MESSAGE IN MOTION

Before class, purchase a bag or two of small powdered sugar donuts. You'll also need vanilla ice cream, chocolate and strawberry toppings, and maraschino cherries. Check with another class leader to see if your class can serve a delicious treat and ask how many kids might be expected. For a change, consider serving an adult class or a youth class.

Set out the plastic spoons, paper bowls, and goodies. Explain that you'll be making super serving treats to serve to the kids (or adults) in another class. To make each treat, place a small donut in a bowl, then add a spoonful of vanilla ice cream. Drizzle either chocolate or strawberry topping over the ice cream, then top it all with a maraschino cherry. Have each child make one treat to eat and one to share. Take the treats to the other class and serve the students and teacher a bit of sweet kindness!

When you're back in the room, read aloud Galatians 5:13b as you enjoy the goodies and chat about how it felt to serve others and about ways you can continue serving others in the coming weeks.

When the treats are nibbled, say: **You've traveled in our church to serve others, so let's add countries to our globe balls that show we can travel around the world to serve!** Add and label Europe and Asia. Say: **We have quite a few countries, but we're not through yet. That's just like serving—no matter** how much we help others, we're never through because it feels so great to serve!

SUPER SCRIPTURE

Form four Scripture teams and hand each team a copy of one of the Mighty Memory Verses from page 127. (If you have older kids, also distribute the corresponding extra challenge verses.) Say: **In this review activity, your team needs to do three things: repeat the verse together for the class, explain what your verse means, and give one reason why this verse helps us serve God and others better. You'll have a few minutes to discuss your answers, then we'll share them with the whole group.**

After several minutes, ask each group to repeat their Mighty Memory Verse, tell what it means, and explain why the verse helps us be good servant leaders.

When all the groups have shared, repeat each verse two times in unison. Then have kids stand in a circle and set their globe balls behind them. Take turns tossing the extra ball to kids in the circle and give them the first three words of a Mighty Memory Verse. Whoever catches the ball completes the verse, then tosses the ball to someone else. Continue giving word clues and tossing the ball until everyone has had a turn repeating a verse.

Say: **These Scripture verses help us learn how God wants us to serve, where he wants us to serve, and whom he wants us to serve. In other words, God wants us to serve others with glad and willing hearts all over the world! And now we can add two last continents to our globe balls to show that we have traveled all around the world!**

Have kids use permanent markers to add Africa. Then have kids place their fingers where Australia should be (several inches to the right of the tip of Africa) and draw a freehand oval to represent Australia. Label Africa and Australia.

Say: **Let's end our day with a prayer to thank God for helping us understand what serving is all about and for guiding us in becoming powerful servant leaders for him.**

A POWERFUL PROMISE

Have children sit in a circle and hold their globe balls. Say: **We've spent several weeks learning about being servant leaders for God. We've explored what being a servant means and the qualities that make a** powerful servant leader. **What are some of those qualities?** Invite kids to tell their ideas. If needed, use the footprints you've been taping to the wall over the past several weeks to give clues.

Say: **We've discovered ways that Jesus taught us to serve and how other men, women, and children in the Bible served God and others. And we've worked on four Mighty Memory Verses that teach us how, where, and whom to serve. Let's bow our heads as I read several Bible verses about serving as a prayer thanking God for his love and guidance in helping us become his faithful servant leaders.** Read aloud the following verses, then end with "amen."

Serve one another in love. (Galatians 5:13)

Serve wholeheartedly, as if you were serving the Lord, not men.
    (Ephesians 6:7)

*And whatever you do, whether in word or deed, do it all in the name
    of the Lord Jesus, giving thanks to God the Father through him.*
    (Colossians 3:17)

*May the Lord make your love increase and overflow for each other
    and for everyone else, just as ours does for you.* (1 Thessalonians
    3:12)

I thank God, whom I serve. (2 Timothy 1:3)

Amen.

Say: **God wants us to serve others, and he promises to help us find ways to serve when our hearts are ready and willing to serve. Let's make a promise to continue to seek ways to serve God and others by being his servant leaders. And to show that we're willing to go to the ends of the earth to serve God, let's draw the North and South Poles on our globe balls as we make a promise and say: "I'll always be your servant leader, Lord."** Pass a marker around the circle until everyone has had a chance to make a promise and quickly draw the North and South Poles.

Say: **Let's end by honoring God with a song. We'll sing "He's Got the Whole World in His Hands" as you gently toss your globe balls up and down in time to the song. Remember that God is in control of the whole world and that he wants us to be his special helpers and servants the whole world over!**

Sing "He's Got the Whole World in His Hands" as kids toss their globe balls up and down. Then end with this responsive good-bye:

Leader: **May you serve God with loving hearts.**

Children: **And also you!**

Remind kids to take home their globe balls and encourage them to keep their promises to God.

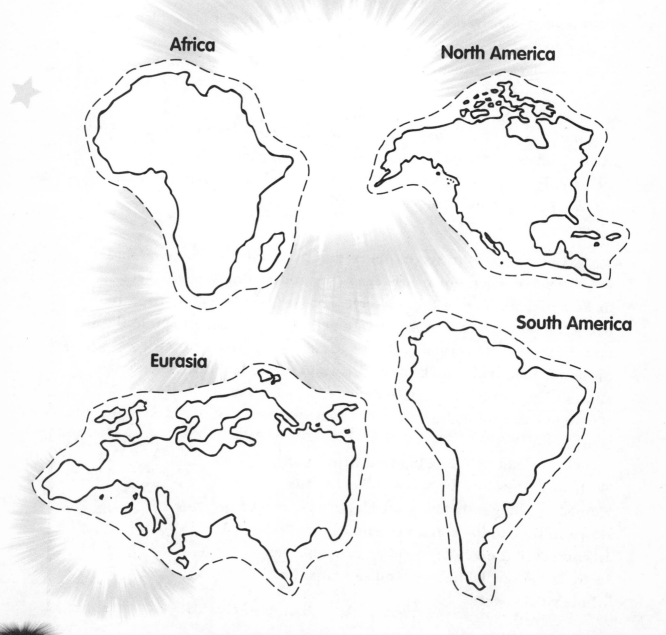

Africa

North America

South America

Eurasia

SWEET SCRIPTURES

Serve one another in love. (Galatians 5:13)

Whatever you do, whether in word or deed, do it all in the name of the Lord Jesus, giving thanks to God the Father through him. (Colossians 3:17)

May he work in us what is pleasing to him, through Jesus Christ. (Hebrews 13:21)

I thank God, whom I serve. (2 Timothy 1:3)

The entire law is summed up in a single command: "Love your neighbor as yourself." (Galatians 5:14)

Serve wholeheartedly, as if you were serving the Lord, not men. (Ephesians 6:7)

COURAGE CARDS

Tell a girl in class, "Jesus loves you, and so do I."

Give someone in class a giant hug.

Sing "Twinkle, Twinkle Little Star."

Show what you look like brushing your teeth.

Recite the alphabet backwards.

Try to do the splits.

Shake a boy's hand.

Thank the leader for being a leader for God!

MISSIONARY SCAVENGER HUNT LISTS

SCHOOL SUPPLIES

These items must be new. They will be used in missionary schools and church services for children.

- ❏ pencils and sharpeners
- ❏ erasers
- ❏ writing tablets
- ❏ drawing paper
- ❏ construction paper
- ❏ clear tape
- ❏ a stapler and staples
- ❏ scissors (adult and kids')
- ❏ crayons and markers
- ❏ paints
- ❏ glue
- ❏ rulers

CLOTHING ITEMS

These items can be new or gently used, but be sure all items are clean and folded. Clothing will be used for villages and others who are in need.

- ❏ socks (all sizes)
- ❏ shirts and sweaters
- ❏ pants
- ❏ caps
- ❏ dresses
- ❏ shoes or slippers
- ❏ belts
- ❏ fabric for sewing
- ❏ needle and thread
- ❏ buttons and snaps
- ❏ jackets

PERSONAL CARE ITEMS

These items must be new and will be used for villages and others who are in need or for the missionaries themselves.

- ❏ combs and brushes
- ❏ toothbrushes
- ❏ toothpaste
- ❏ hand soap
- ❏ lotion
- ❏ shampoo
- ❏ dental floss
- ❏ adhesive bandages
- ❏ antiseptic cream
- ❏ bug repellent
- ❏ sunscreen lotion
- ❏ towels or washcloths

BIBLES-N-BOOKS

These items can be new or gently used. They'll be enjoyed by children and adults, so picture books as well as easy readers are wonderful.

- ❏ Bibles (for all ages)
- ❏ Bible storybooks
- ❏ Bible activity books
- ❏ Bible story coloring books
- ❏ puzzles and puzzle books
- ❏ animal story books
- ❏ Christmas stories
- ❏ hymnals
- ❏ song books
- ❏ Easter storybooks
- ❏ Bible studies

GOOD NEWS NEWSPAPER

KIDS GO FOR GOD IN GREAT WAYS!

HUG HELPS THE HURT

A little girl who recently lost her father to lightning received a hug of love from a ten-year-old who sent the toddler a tiny stuffed cat. The ten-year-old used his allowance to buy the gift because he knew how sad the little girl was over the loss of her "daddy." The toddler had received burns from the lightning accident, and when doctors bandaged her leg with pink bandages, her little stuffed friend was bandaged, too. The toddler's family said she won't go anywhere without the stuffed cat. When asked why he wanted to help a toddler he didn't know, the ten-year-old said, "They say money can't buy happiness, but I think it bought a hug!"

WHO was served?

_____

HOW were they served?

_____

TEXAS TEACHER ALL SMILES

A group of elementary school kids in Texas learned that their favorite teacher was retiring. This teacher had helped many kids for over twenty years with their homework, their math lessons, and even their troubles. The kids wanted to make sure their teacher wouldn't forget how special she was even if they weren't there to tell her. These clever kids sold pencils for a nickel apiece and made enough money to purchase their teacher-friend a beautiful paperweight— and a heart full of smiles and memories!

WHO was served?

_____

HOW were they served?

_____

TREES PLEASE!

One stormy day in Nebraska, a big wind blew over several trees that had only hours before shaded kids playing on swings and enjoying cool picnics. This favorite play place, many kids thought, looked lonesome and bare without trees, so they decided to do something about it. Several kids sold lemonade, a few sold old toys, and others went door to door with ten-cents-for-a-tree cans. After several weeks of hard work, they collected enough money to buy two small trees from a local nursery. When the nursery discovered what the trees were for, they donated another pair of trees to the park project. Just like leaves on trees, good turns blossomed and multiplied for this lucky park and the people who enjoy it!

WHO was served?

_____

HOW were they served?

_____

FOOTPRINT PATTERN

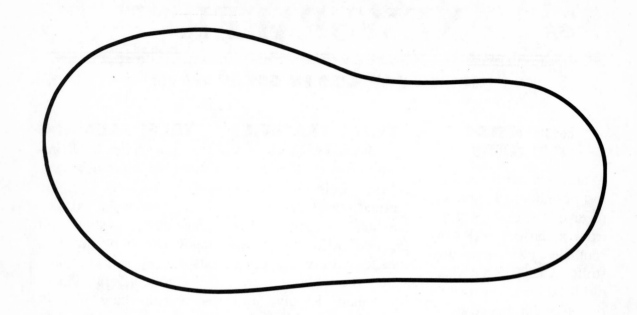

GIFT CARDS

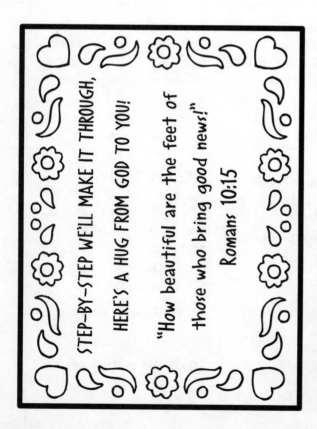

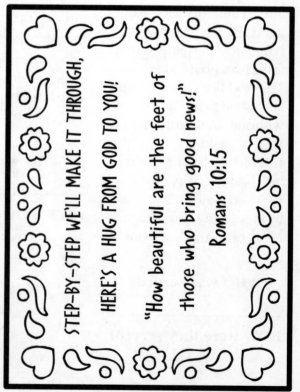

STEP-BY-STEP WE'LL MAKE IT THROUGH,

HERE'S A HUG FROM GOD TO YOU!

"How beautiful are the feet of those who bring good news!"

Romans 10:15

SCRIPTURE STRIPS

Whatever you do, work at it with all your heart, as working for the Lord, not for men. *Colossians 3:23*

Serve one another in love. *Galatians 5:13b*

And we know that in all things God works for the good of those who love him, who have been called according to his purpose. *Romans 8:28*

Whoever serves me must follow me; and where I am, my servant also will be. My Father will honor the one who serves me. *John 12:26*

I tell you the truth, whatever you did for one of the least of these brothers of mine, you did for me. *Matthew 25:40*

You see that his faith and his actions were working together, and his faith was made complete by what he did. *James 2:22*

Therefore go and make disciples of all nations, baptizing them in the name of the Father and of the Son and of the Holy Spirit. *Matthew 28:19*

And teaching them to obey everything I have commanded you. And surely I am with you always, to the very end of the age. *Matthew 28:20*